# OCEAN OF SELF-LOVE

IT IS LIMITLESS…

ASHA NAIR

**Xpress**Publishing
An imprint of Notion Press

No.8, 3rd Cross St, CIT Colony,
Mylapore, Chennai,
Tamil Nadu - 600004

First Published by Notion Press 2020
Copyright © ASHA NAIR 2020
All Rights Reserved.

ISBN 978-1-63633-439-4

This book has been published with all efforts taken to make the material error-free after the consent of the author. However, the author and the publisher do not assume and hereby disclaim any liability to any party for any loss, damage, or disruption caused by errors or omissions, whether such errors or omissions result from negligence, accident, or any other cause.

While every effort has been made to avoid any mistake or omission, this publication is being sold on the condition and understanding that neither the author nor the publishers or printers would be liable in any manner to any person by reason of any mistake or omission in this publication or for any action taken or omitted to be taken or advice rendered or accepted on the basis of this work. For any defect in printing or binding the publishers will be liable only to replace the defective copy by another copy of this work then available.

*Dedicated to my wonderful husband, Arun.*

*Thank you for a life time of love, support and inspiration..*

# Contents

| | |
|---|---|
| Preface | 9 |
| Acknowledgments | 13 |
| Chapter 01 | 15 |
|    A BETTER ME | 17 |
|    A PROMISE TO SELF | 23 |
|    AN ALLY CALLED SELF-BELIEF | 25 |
| Chapter 02 | 33 |
|    BE YOURSELF AND JUST BE | 35 |
|    BE AWARE OF YOUR OWN SELF | 41 |
|    BOOST YOUR CONFIDENCE | 47 |
|    BUILD YOUR SELF-ESTEEM | 54 |
|    BE YOUR OWN BEST FRIEND | 58 |
| Chapter 03 | 61 |
|    CULTIVATE CONSISTENCY | 63 |
| Chapter 04 | 69 |
|    DISCOVER YOURSELF | 71 |
|    DEFINE YOURSELF | 77 |
|    DATE WITH THE SELF | 80 |

# CONTENTS

| | |
|---|---|
| Chapter 05 | 85 |
|   EMBRACE YOURSELF | **87** |
|   EMBRACE YOUR FLAWS | **91** |
| Chapter 06 | 95 |
|   FIND YOUR CALLING | **97** |
| Chapter 07 | 101 |
|   GIFTS TO GIVE YOURSELF | **103** |
| Chapter 08 | 109 |
|   HEAL YOURSELF | **111** |
| Chapter 09 | 119 |
|   I AM POSSIBLE | **121** |
| Chapter 10 | 127 |
|   JUST LAUGH IT AWAY | **129** |
| Chapter 11 | 135 |
|   KNOW(ING)! THE SELF | **137** |
| Chapter 12 | 145 |
|   LIVING WITH THE REAL YOU | **147** |
|   LIVE BEFORE YOU LEAVE | **153** |
|   LIFT YOURSELF BY YOURSELF | **159** |
| Chapter 13 | 165 |
|   MAKE YOURSELF COUNT | **167** |
| Chapter 14 | 175 |
|   NATURE NURTURES SELF | **177** |
| Chapter 15 | 183 |
|   OCEAN AND I | **185** |

| | |
|---|---|
| Chapter 16 | 189 |
|     **PUTTING YOURSELF FIRST IS NOT SELFISH** | **191** |
| Chapter 17 | 197 |
|     **QUALITY CONSCIOUSNESS** | **199** |
| Chapter 18 | 203 |
|     **RUN YOUR OWN RACE** | **205** |
| Chapter 19 | 211 |
|     **STAND UP FOR YOURSELF** | **213** |
| Chapter 20 | 227 |
|     **TAME YOUR TRIGGERS** | **229** |
|     **THE BEST VERSION OF ME** | **234** |
| Chapter 21 | 249 |
|     **UPGRADE YOURSELF** | **251** |
| Chapter 22 | 255 |
|     **VALUE YOURSELF** | **257** |
|     **VICTORY OVER YOURSELF** | **263** |
| Chapter 23 | 267 |
|     **WONDER YOURSELF** | **269** |
| Chapter 24 | 275 |
|     **XESTURGY OF YOUR INNER SELF** | **277** |
| Chapter 25 | 279 |
|     **YOUR WORDS CREATE YOUR WORLD** | **281** |
| Chapter 26 | 287 |
|     **ZEN AND THE SELF** | **289** |

# Preface

*"Self-love is an ocean and your heart is a vessel. Make it full, and any excess will spill over into the lives of the people you hold dear. But you must come first."*

*— Beau Taplin*

This book is about 'Self-love' just what the title says. In one sense, this book is a key to a complete life. It is about YOU and FOR YOU. All creations of your life, manifestations of your dreams and all attainment of your happiness, begins with YOU. If you need someone's love in the World then It's only from YOU... If you need respect then also it's from YOU. The entire A to Z of life depends on the most defining factor "love of self" in shaping the kind of life you live. So it's time for you to immerse yourself in the ocean of "Self-Love". In another sense, this book is thinking outside the box. It is omitting limitations and that is exactly what some effective and innovative kind of thinking does. No one in this world can make you happy. You need to like yourself and achieve happiness within. Polish the mirror of your life, such that one day you begin to see clearly, who you are. That is getting in touch with the Creative 'Self' releases tremendous energy. It also boosts confidence, helps you find more equilibrium and a sense of well-being as well as a chain effect on other areas of your life. Our true

'Self' is our heart. In order to like yourself, you need to embrace your positive aspects and divide your negative aspects into two groups. Some bad points can be changed and other one that cannot. Just imagine if you are five feet and you don't like it, so sorry! You have to deal with that flaws. When you love yourself, it wouldn't matter how the model in the advertisement looks like. You will never come across a fine work of art and machinery like your body. You are the most original and authentic work of art that you can rely on. To truly experience this, we should let go of our default tendency to prove ourselves when provoked and express our originality despite the provocations. We all have our own stories and are different personalities, none higher or lower than the others. If we miss ourselves in this life time, we miss this life time itself. We accept or reject anything or anybody. However, our likes and dislikes do not matter to the world. If you can't find your soul, then it will be difficult to find others. We have to accept ourselves with our weaknesses and strengths.

## The PURSUIT OF 'SELF-LOVE'

Life is a series of relationships. The primary relationship is intra-relationship — your relationship with 'YOURSELF'. You can give, what you have. If you have ignorance, you can give only your ignorance. If you have wisdom, then you can give only your wisdom. If you can't stand for yourself, you will not be able to stand for anymore. If you don't accept yourself for what you are, you will not be able to accept for what others are. If you define yourself by your looks, you will judge the world by its looks. If you define yourself by your character, you will judge the world by its character. If you don't love yourself, then you cannot love others. Thus, the world you perceive is just a reflection of how you perceive yourself. When you love yourself, you attract better version of yourself. You let the Universe know that you deserve the best by treating yourself well.

Everything starts with how you feel about yourself... Feel worthy... Feel valuable... Feel special... Feel deserving of receiving the BEST... Feel your full spectrum of emotions and acknowledge what makes you human. Be in love with 'YOURSELF' and let the Whole Universe be in love with you. When you fall in love with yourself immensely, respect yourself immeasurably and inspire yourself infinitely... the whole Universe will fall in love with you... people can't stop admiring you... people cannot stop respecting you... and you stay in complete peace, love, and humility... because your happiness comes from within. Watch yourself blossom. Find your flow with the Universe and ride that energetic waves wherever it may lead. The Waves of the Universe whispered in silence. "Love thyself to love thy Universe. Seamlessly, calmly, gently, cross thy barriers and let love loose to gush all around you". Oh, how true! The Universe has taught us — unconditional 'Self-love' is the answer to loving one and all.

# Acknowledgments

'Ocean of Self-love' was a team effort. It would not have been possible to complete without the help of family members and few friends. First and foremost, my husband Arun, for organising my life and making sure that I had time to work on the book. Then, my sons Ankit and Abhinav, who never ceased to believe in me and supported me throughout the entire process. My sincere thanks goes to my mother for her love and support. I am thankful to a friend Preethi Ramachandran for her love and helpful feedback.

I would like to acknowledge Dr. Sunil Awana, Sr. Consultant Neuro Psychiatrist for his encouragement in my personal transformational steps. In particular, I am grateful to the spiritual master, healer and hypnotherapist, Shri Amit Manocha who simply states the essence of the human condition in a profound and inspiring way. I also wish to express my gratitude to Shri Dharampal Bajaj, who have selflessly enriched and motivated me in many ways beyond measure.

Many examples, anecdotes are the result of a collection from various sources, such as newspapers, magazines and blogs over the last 15 years. I wish to express my gratitude to those sources who have contributed to this work. It has been a pleasure to work with Notion Press, and the cooperation of the editorial and production staff is much appreciated. I'll forever be grateful for all of your input in my life.

## Chapter 01
# A BETTER ME
# A PROMISE TO SELF
# AN ALLY CALLED SELF BELIEF

# A BETTER ME

*"Do the best you can until you know better. Then when you know better, do better."*

— *Maya Angelou*

In this world of upgrading we are obsessed in upgrading everything right. We have upgraded our houses, school curriculums, music systems, cameras, mobiles, the category of flights we take and the apps. With every upgrade, the older version loses its value and the newer version gains all the importance and adulation. I sometimes wonder whether I should ever upgrade myself and I feel dire need to do this. There should be a constant upgrading process. Only then can we feel the freshness and newness as every time we shed some of our bad habits and imbibe some good ones. The beauty of life is in its unpredictability. Hence it is better to make the best use of a given point in time, though something else always looks better.

Procrastination is a trait that varies extremely; some people don't suffer from it at all, being constantly busy and efficient, while others find it rules their lives. They are constantly putting off until tomorrow what they should do today. Procrastination typically react to pressure by balking and becoming even worse. Then one day you will wake up and there won't be any time to do things you've always wanted to do. Why put off improving yourself? Do it now?

Life is all about striving to do our best always. Perhaps it is also about striking the right balance. Yes, it is possible to get the best of the worlds, but we need to consciously make an effort to make that possible. I decided to give my best to whatever I do. I want to see a new version of me, a better version of me with a thirst for continuous self-improvement. It is important to stop judging and to end struggle with yourself, generally on the grounds of laziness, anxiety and self-doubt. Ask positive, action-oriented questions: How do I stop procrastinating and postponing? *vs.* How can I be proactive and do everything on time? The question may sound similar but you will get different answers.

## BE A BETTER YOU, FOR YOU

*"When opportunity presents itself grab it. Hold on tight and don't let it go."*

— *Celia Cruz*

Most of the times we don't realise what we are made up of. What is our essential property? What is the purpose for which each of us are here? What impressions and impact are we going to leave behind? What will we be remembered for? Adversity comes into our lives to teach us and show us what are we made of. Do we succumb to the pressure of life or do we emerge victorious beyond the odds? We need to delve deep and understand ourselves. What should be our attitude towards life in those feeble moments. Let's go to Derek's example and gain maturity out of it...

During the Barcelona Olympics 1992, in the 400-meter sprint, when Derek Redmond was injured with a torn hamstring, the rational move would have been to lie down on the stretcher and be carried out of the stadium terming it a medical emergency. If he had opted for this logical move, it would have been recorded as an event in history and forgotten. But, Derek Redmond, being a world champion, choose to finish the race despite the injury. Seeing Derek in pain and agony, his father came running to help him and carry him through his race. His message to his son was

George Bernard Shaw's quote: *"Life is no brief candle to me. It is a sort of splendid torch which I have got a hold of for the moment, and I want to make it burn as brightly as possible before handling it on future generations."* He received a standing ovation from over 65, 000 people. By choosing not to give up, and still completing the race with the injury, battling pain and the agony of the torn hamstring, he made the event an inspirational record in times to come. This moment is what we call an epiphany - where an ordinary person becomes a history maker, a reference point in the history of mankind.

Life presents such moments which occur only once in our lifetime. These moments have the power to change the core of who we are. They say that such epiphany can happen to everyone... Then why is that only a few become legends and achieve greatness? It's because most of us don't even know an epiphany has occurred in our lives. We let the moment pass away by not being alert or not being in the present moment. We choose what's convenient to do rather than let the churning develop and change the core of who we are. Limits exits only in our mind. Life is a bottomless pit- that's the definition that befits life. The message is loud and clear - "We can be better than what we are right now!"

## I AM HAPPY TO BE ME

*"No matter who you are, no matter what you did, no matter where you've come from, you can always change, become a better version of yourself."*

— *Madonna*

To have strength in your own convictions, helps you to lead a happier life. Convictions, or the principles which we hold on to, have the essential power to build strength in us and keeps us growing. They help us to be comfortable with our own selves at all times and in all states. The whole process starts with our thoughts, which could either be self-induced, self-inculcated or instilled in us by others whom we look up to. These thoughts with constant repetition over and over again, convert themselves into affirmations which on further repetitions become beliefs. A belief, over a period of time, sets in as strong deep-rooted convictions.

My conviction always brings me hope regardless of the outcome. It is something so intrinsically a part of my own self. It is like an approval to myself that all my actions are the result of my deep thoughts which I believe in to be right and true, helping me to accept myself irrespective of the results. Above all, I assume and accept responsibility for the action, the all direct future actions... and I can still be happy and approving of myself. There is less need over a period of time to get the approval of others. In fact, the desire for approval is nil. I have become responsible for both my actions and inactions. To live with a conviction sends an expanded thought to your inner self. Convictions have a gratifying effect and form a conduit between the inner self and the world a connect between what you wish to look at and what you see. Convictions have the power to inspire one's dreams and supply enough energy to achieve the same. Conan O'Brien rightly said, *"With clarity comes conviction and true originality."* True enough... a conviction is that which comes with clarity of mind and thought which leads to rightful and directed action. Convictions give courage and strong ability to move forward. One such conviction which I firmly believe in is that 'I AM HAPPY TO BE ME'.

One day, I was swallowed, in an encumbering state of mind, a spark lit up my thoughts - What is my one dominant dream towards which parts of my desires should focus upon? The parts are not my dream. But how I integrate the parts to whole is my dream. Doubts. Fear and uncertainty are parts of my dream as well, just that they are unwelcome. Even if I ignore them, their presence is real. They are here inside me. Dreams can't exist without doubts, fears, uncertainties obstacles and hesitations. It is living through convictions that my attitude gets shaped and preserved. The conviction of approving and affirming one's self gives one immense power to cross all barriers set by society and individual progressively and positively. The convictions have the power of improving self-worth and self-esteem, it acts as a balm, a catalyst and a moderator. It aids in strengthening the inner self, giving one the power to push forward and raise towards one's dream.

This crazy thing called conviction! How to catch it in this fleeting life? All the expressions that I wished to hear were all within me and I feel the whole world now approves of me even without asking for it. Thanks to my conviction, I feel all the thoughts and action to be so directed. I feel empowered and as a result, I am able to send ripples of my positive mindset and vibrations to people whom I come in contact with. One strong lesson I have understood about life and from life is: if we hold on to our convictions, stick to the principles we believe in to be true long enough, hard enough and strong enough, nothing can shake us and at the same time, we should conduct ourselves respectfully and honourably in line with what we believe in to be true. My conviction has helped me to be more confident, self-approving, self-ratifying above all, bereft of assumptions and self-deception. The self-approval gave happiness to my inner self, and most importantly the absence of self-deceit gave roots to my convictions. So, the result is bliss, a happier self.

If you want a happier world and happier self in your life, learn to live with a conviction which in turn have a gratifying effect between the inner self and the world outside... Changing our thought patterns will help us channelize our energy and our life will change accordingly. The way you see the people and the people around you, are a reflection of your own thought process and hence the happier self helps us to see a happier world. The thought process of a person is what feeds the good or bad. And owing to this, the incidents around seem so much simpler. Convictions also helps to keep oneself away from unproductive remarks and debates.

*I love myself the way I am;*
*I love myself for what I am;*
*I love myself for who I am;*
*I love myself for where I am;*
*I love myself whatever I am;*
*I love myself however I am;*
*I love myself since I am work in progress;*
*I am happy to be me and waiting to meet 'my better me'.*

# A PROMISE TO SELF

*"The worst promise you can break is the one you make to yourself."*

— David Kirsch

A promise is a powerful expression of yourself.

So, what is a promise?

P — personal feeling
R — rationalism
O — optimization
M — moralization
I — interpretation
S — sagacity
E — energy

The word 'Promise' is a personal feeling, something that we make to ourselves. It is something we follow strictly by rationalising our behaviour. As a result, it makes us very optimistic above our own actions or behaviour. Thus, we moralise our values which gives us insight into ourselves. This in turn generates a positive energy within.

A few months back whenever I got into a heated argument with my parents or friends, I would always raise my voice to win the argument. During those days, I never regretted my behaviour until I realised one day that I was winning the argument but not my loved one's heart. From then I promised to myself that I must stop behaving in this manner.

I pulled out a notebook and designated it as my mood tracker notebook. I drew a big circle and divide it into 30/31 equal parts (depending on the number of days for each month) like a pie diagram. Then I started tracking my moods. On days when I was angry, I would mark that day in red, on days when I was calm or relaxed, I would mark it in green.

I made a promise to myself that I should not see a single red mark on the page for three months and I succeeded. On the other side if you are constantly making and breaking promises to yourself, you're not making promises at all, you are saying.

Raising your voice in anger serves to only distance you from the person you love. Like all other emotions, anger too has both negative and positive aspects. However, what sets this emotion apart is that its radius of impact is the widest of all. Instead of getting absorbed in your anger, observe as this emotion starts to overpower you. Express anger not unleash it. Accept anger; do not suppress it. Guide it; do not follow it. Whatever be the intensity of the emotion, always be aware of it.

When milk boils over; we need to switch off the gas stove; when emotions boil over we need to switch off our voice. Stay silent when you are angry, keep calm and stay positive. Just for today, understand your anger. Befriend it.

A promise helps us to evolve... It follows that it is the highest importance to be sure that the self on which we stake all our hopes and aspirations is really the truest and deepest side of self. By expressing the right amount of emotions at the right time for the right cause, one can unleash a lot of creative power for one's own and the community's good. Remember God is always silent... Promise yourself today to be so strong that nothing can disturb your peace of mind.

# AN ALLY CALLED SELF-BELIEF

The journey is never easy, nothing comes easy for anyone. The people who make it to top did not have an easy time reaching there. It takes a lot of sacrifice, focus, devotion, determination and an enormous amount of self-belief to get to top. Belief is what you have in yourself. As you sow, so you reap. As you think, so you become. Your beliefs create your reality. You are moulting when you trust others belief in you. But you are rebirthing when you believe in yourself.

- **YOU ARE WHAT YOU BELIEVE**

    *"Magic is believing in yourself, if you can do that, you can make anything happen."*

    — Johann Wolfgang Von Goethe

The most important quality you can ever develop is having belief in yourself. Many people wish they could accomplish certain things but lack the belief that they actually do it. Each one of us has feeling of inferiority because we feel we are not good enough to acquire and enjoy things we want in life. Often, we feel that we don't deserve good things. The Universal law of Belief says that whatever we believe, with feeling becomes our reality. We don't believe what we see; instead we see what we believe. Our belief forms a screen as to how we see the world, and we never allow any information that is not consistent with our beliefs to pass through it. Your attitude, skills and knowledge are mere means for the fulfilment of your beliefs. Your beliefs precede and superimpose all other factors. To be rich, you got to believe you deserve to be rich. To be healthy, you got to believe you can be healthy. You cannot outperform your beliefs. Either you can perform to your beliefs, or you might underperform to your beliefs. So, if you want to alter your life, you must alter your beliefs. Your life will expand only when your beliefs expand. Your life shrinks when your belief shrinks. Your beliefs are the check post through which your future manifests. Rationalists would say, "When I see it, only then will I believe it". But the fact is, "Only when you believe in it, you will see it." Your life is a reflection of your beliefs.

- **SELF-LIMITING BELIEFS**

The most common and also the most harmful beliefs are the ones that are self-limiting. These are beliefs about yourself. Virtually every person has the capacity to do wonderful things with his or her life. But the greatest single obstacles for most people is self-doubt. Self-limiting beliefs act as breaks on our ability to achieve our goals. Many of us have hopes, dreams and aspirations, but we let doubts creep in and undermine our talents, abilities and effectiveness. For example, believing that you can't achieve something because you don't have enough money or education. You might believe you can't achieve something because you are the wrong sex, race, age or it is because of the economy. Most of these beliefs are not true, they will hold you back nonetheless.

Rain fills the size of the vessel. Whether your life is filled with scarcity or adequacy or abundance depends on the size of your beliefs. Ordinary people, when they hold on to extraordinary beliefs, become extraordinary people. You don't become Mahatma Gandhi and then start believing in your power to shape the destiny of a nation. When you are still Mohandas Gandhi, you believe in your power and potential to lead a revolution, and that results in the becoming of a Mahatma. The only real limitation on what you can be and have, is if you lack the desire.

- **STOP MAKING EXCUSES**

Do you hear yourself saying? When I have enough money, I'll...When I go on vacation. I'll... As soon as I find the right partner, I'll... When the house is clean. I'll be able to... When I can afford a better car, I'll... When this project is over, I'll... As soon I get more clients, I'll... When my kids are grown and moved out, I'll... How much of your life you put on hold? The most popular justification people give are that they are waiting for the money or the time to magically open up. However, we are not hungry enough to do what it takes to find or create the future. There are five elements when achieving prosperity. Money is only one of them. Energy (sometimes mislabeled as power), love, time and success are the other four. Beliefs underlies this whole process. The belief that you need money to accomplish whatever is on your list. The belief that there are no other options.

And so many more. What are your beliefs that are placing your "I'll's" on your hold list? Until you are aware of what's on your list and they are a true want, you don't open up your vision to their possibilities. Ask new questions when your beliefs sabotage your success. This is examining that belief. When this occurs, it is important to ask this valuable question: What is the belief? You need to name it to claim it. Many times, we don't want to own that belief— we avoid the ownership. This denial dances around until we can no longer stay behind the way. Hence learn to name it, this automatically starts the change, then take it one step at a time from that point. If your life is full of excuses, there isn't any room. Take a leap of faith purposely every day for the next week. When it works, continue the process. Even if you cannot run ahead of others, dare to run completely in a right direction of your intelligence to build a strong-belief.

- **HOW TO DEVELOP POSITIVE BELIEFS**

*"Without self-belief nothing can be accomplished, with it, nothing is impossible."*

— Felix Dennis

To develop positive beliefs, you have to decide exactly where you want to end up in future. The clearer you are about the result you want to end up in your future, the easier it will be for you to change your actions and behaviours in the short term. This in turn, will assure that you achieve what you want in the long term. Once you've clearly decided on the type of person you want to be you will have already taken a major first step in developing new positive beliefs. In order to incorporate your new beliefs into your everyday life, you have to discipline yourself to act exactly in every situation as if you already were that person. When you begin to act like the successful person, you will actually adopt their values, qualities, and characteristics. And that positive beliefs become a permanent part of your personality. Your attitude will change and become more positive. If you consistently act like the person you want to become every day and in every situation, it will become a chain reaction. This will then build stronger and more positive beliefs. And your beliefs will then exert a positive influence on your values. You are a good person from this day forward, see yourself as the very best you can be, and refuse to accept any limitation on your possibilities. Once you develop that belief in yourself and you act in accordance with your beliefs, your future will be unlimited.

- **RESOURCES NEEDED TO FULFIL DREAMS**
  When people think about pursuing something, they first take a look at their resources to determine whether or not they can do it. But where most people fall in this process is when they look at their resources, they are usually taking stock of the wrong resources. Most people immediately look at money. But money is not the

greatest resource. In fact, there are other resources that are more important than money.

1) Desire: Everything that comes from life comes from wanting it. Really wanting it. Do you have desire in you for something? A fire in the belly that cannot be put out no matter what? Do you have this kind of desire for what you seek? Then you will accomplish it.

2) Vision: Robert Schuller once said, *"You never have a money problem, only a vision problem."* Well said. If you have vision for something, you will attract the money needed. Vision is that grand spectacular plan that sees the big picture, paints it for others, and draws them along. Do you have a vision for what it is you want to accomplish? Can you see it even if it isn't here yet? Can you hear it? Smell it?

3) Persistence: The great myth of successful people is that they are just more talented. But this simply isn't true in most cases. It may not be glamorous, but the fact is that most people get ahead of the pack by simply trying harder, working longer, doing more, and basically just persisting longer than the average failure. Do you persist when the going gets tough? When it looks like the goal will be a little further off and a little longer in arriving do you quit and go elsewhere or do you buckle down and attack with more diligence.

4) Guts, courage, bravery, nerve, valour. Do you have them? Can you look risk in the eye and not blink? The

men and women of this world who have accomplish tremendous things were not handed those things. I have found that every single one of them had moments of pure unadulterated fear. But what separated them from the rest is that they had the guts to go forward anyway. When others slunk off into the distance, they forged ahead.

In short, belief is what you have in yourself. You can utilise your potential only to the extent you believe in yourself. Great people achieved greatness because, they believed in themselves. It's not about whether the world believes in you or not, you got to believe yourself. Look into your beliefs, transform your beliefs and design your own destiny.

## Chapter 02
# BE YOURSELF AND JUST BE
# BE AWARE OF YOURSELF
# BOOST YOUR CONFIDENCE
# BUILD YOUR SELF-ESTEEM
# BE YOUR OWN BEST FRIEND

# BE YOURSELF AND JUST BE

*"Be yourself. Everyone else is already taken."*

— *Oscar Wilde*

I am a person who stands for a breakthrough for humanity. I stand for human magnificence. I stand for our ability to be source-creators, to evolve life and to evolve ourselves into mega-beings of great passion, wisdom, wonder and possibility. To forget completely who we are, and to have to face a life where you might possibly never remember, is an act of the deepest bravery and courage I can imagine. To face every day, the slings and arrows of the 'real 'world, that for some reason just does't seem to know you and accept you for the wonderful being that you are. How many of you are walking around with that mega-you inside of you, hidden away safely so it can't get trampled on one more time? How many of you are hiding behind a mask of something that's not really you? Humbleness? Fierceness? Coldness? Warm-heartedness? There are lots of reasons to keep wearing them. Well, I say it's time to come out of the closet? Time to throw away those masks and be truly everything, you really, genuinely are! Don't be afraid of your passion, of your power, of your knowing of yourself. Being true to yourself, to your passions and vision is, the place where the dance of evolution begins.

## POWER OF POSSIBILITY THINKING

*"If you open yourself up to possibility thinking, you open yourself up to many other possibilities."*

— *Lukman Sowunmi*

There is nothing more empowering than possibility thinking, especially if you are stuck in a situation which you cannot change. As you delve into possibility thinking, you are compelled to pull yourself out of the quagmire of your current mental and emotional state and access a higher frequency of consciousness. A place where things happen. Possibility thinking starts with the conviction that you make a difference, that you are capable of doing greater and greater things. Searching for possibilities that may be right under one's nose. These possibilities become apparent when we reconfigure our interpretation of a situation or look at an old situation with new eyes, using an opportunistic thinking style. When people do not want to give up on their dreams, possibility thinking takes birth. Very often, it is the process of intense inner churning that compels people to leave the beaten track and look for alternative solutions. For instance, Sophia Roy a shamanic healer, past life regression therapist and clairvoyant from Hyderabad. Her mother had died at child birth. Her hopes of finding love and acceptance were shattered by the cruelty and indifference of her stepmother towards her. She felt that she was living on the periphery as an uncomfortable add-on to the family of her father, stepmother and their daughter. In the scenario, she considered nature as her mother and she was happiest in its lap. Her father's army job ensured acres of land and big British houses populated with trees, flowers, insects, and animals. Marriage happened early at the age of eighteen. However, the gaping wounds of insecurity and loveless life could not be filled by marriage. The deep pain made her wonder about her state and seek answers in spirituality. It was at that time she met Dr. Newton Kondaveti and his wife Dr. Lakshmi, famous past life regression therapists from India. Through them, she understood how only she could love herself. She worked on many methodologies and became a certified past life regression therapist herself.

## AN OPEN MIND CREATES POSSIBILITIES

*"If you embrace possibility thinking, your dreams will go from molehill to mountain size, and because you believe in possibilities, you put yourself in position to achieve them."*

— *John. C. Maxwell*

So, what does it mean to have an open mind? It is the act of walking naked into the ocean of infectious possibilities. It is an adventure and, like all adventures, it involves risk. If we take a close look at famous people or any person who has reached the peak of his or her success, you will find one thing in common and similar in everyone's life. We all know that they would have taken THE DECISION in life, the life changing decision which involves a risk factor. A quote comes to mind - *"If you are not willing to risk the unusual, you will have to settle for ordinary."* We all want to achieve something in life. We all have dreams, goals, ambitions and desires to perform, produce and fulfil. We would have heard a lot of times about how, in order to actualise your desires and dreams to reality, you need a sturdy mind, patience, hard work and dedication. Like adding spice gives a meaningful flavour to food, decision making add spice to our goals and path to our dreams. The decision making is that risk factor which gives us courage to do the impossible and the desired. For instance, when you don't take a risk or a chance to grab the opportunity or to make an opportunity for yourself, you lose. You lose the joy and essence of dream path. We may not regret taking a risk, but we will regret not taking a risk. Because, by not taking the decision, we miss an opportunity given to us. Taking a risk may end up in failure. But failure also teach us a lesson. If that decision turns out a success, then it's a life changing one.

Right now, I am thinking of Judy [not her real name]: married life tested her patience by all means while enriching her as a woman by blessing her with a 'fairy'. Since her birth she nurtured a dream to educate her well and make her bold enough to tackle the ups and downs of life courageously. She was just living her personal as well as professional life as it was four years back. Things were neither in her control nor were they controlling her. She was frustrated and torn. Her work place - an educational institution - was less of a place of learning and more of a business world with corrupt strategies. She found herself dissatisfied to the core but kept on giving her utmost. Her personal life was the stereotypical Indian one where her in-laws wished to have things their way without paying any heed to her concerns or desires. Something went terribly wrong at her work place, she had to wrong at her workplace, she had to think of making a change. At both home and work, life was suffocating and unbearable for her. Though she did not join another organisation, she strongly felt that it wasn't her final destination. She believed she had to wait for another door to open. She was half-hearted doing her job, unhappy and detached to an extent because she wasn't contented as her soul was in misery. She wanted a place of peace where human values were respected, and humanity prevailed. She continued to work over there for five long months until a day when, looking at her dissatisfied state, one of her colleagues advised her to think of something bigger and make a move. She told her to apply to a renowned institution in her hometown and that too, in a state far away from hers. As luck would have it, the next day she received a call from the institution and within a few days, she had the appointment letter in her hands. She didn't knew from where she had gathered the courage to tell her family that she was all prepared to leave the city with her eight-year-old daughter to a faraway place which was completely unknown to her. She hadn't ever gone out of station alone but here she was all set to make a move to a strange place! With some unknown conviction, she began to move ahead, step by step. She travelled approximately three thousand kilometers in the hope of initiating an altogether new life! Every face was different. But something sustained her. Her daughter moved to her campus and she got engrossed in her field of work. The place compiled with her dream world where a work culture that resonated with her prevailed; humanity was valued, and an overall system existed. It was no doubt tough to be far away from family, everybody acknowledged her courageous step of moving out of her comfort zone. By and large, we hesitate to take risks; we settle for lesser things, dreading paths unknown. But if we take risks, it brings tremendous change in our life. Her decision had many risks, unacceptability, unsuitability, unfamiliarity, dissatisfaction, loss of self-respect and so much more but it worked out gradually. It is not the end of her journey as she knew that this road will lead to something else. Despite dreaming big and working hard for her dream, she has never reached her finishing line. She has always got stuck somewhere in the middle of race. She settled for the ordinary. She thought of all the ways to succeed and fulfil the desired goal. She failed miserably. When she read about taking risks and decision making something hit hard. She took a look at her past actions, at those that she had taken to fulfil her dream. The picture became clear. Courage was missing. She feared to step out of her boundary. She never risked anything to accomplish what she desired. She was waiting for the food to be fed. Instead of making an opportunity for herself, she was waiting for a journey of roses. If

I look back on my life, whatever risks I have taken till date may not have had positive outcomes, but I feel a kind of satisfaction that my intentions at those junctures of my life were genuine and pure. At times, the internal push or voice of consciousness guides you well and if followed, you are able to breathe in air of contentment. At times, I do become apprehensive wondering if I did right or wrong by making the shift, but when I reassure myself that all my efforts were not 'signalled green' by the Almighty so I need to surrender myself to Him because when He is with us no one can be against us. He makes us do certain things that leave us in utter surprise as to how we could have done it! I conclude by saying – 'Be true to yourself.' - and keep treading the path with a belief in the supreme plan of the Almighty.

> Where you are today
> Is no accident
> God is using the situation
> You are in right now.......
> To shape you and prepare you,
> For the place He wants to bring you into tomorrow;
> Trust Him with His plan even if you don't understand.
> Someone once said, "Fear is temporary, regret is forever".
> Overcoming fear that's what I plan to do.

# BE AWARE OF YOUR OWN SELF

"*The cave you fear to enter holds the treasure you seek"*

*- Joseph Campbell*

We always know 'what to do 'before the incident. We also know 'what we should have done 'after the incident. Yet, our knowledge betrays us during the incident. We continue to behave governed by our habitual patterns. Why is transformation... transcending the old formation such a difficult task? We seem to have solutions for all the problems in the world but we aren't able to solve our own problems. Why? There is no dearth of knowledge in any of us. In fact, there is excessive accumulation of knowledge. The irony is that our knowledge is running parallel to our experiences. There seems to be no meeting point. To achieve that meeting point is called transformation. Integration of knowledge into experiences is called maturity. And maturity is attained through self-awareness. One of the greatest blessings of being human is this gift of self-awareness.

## SELF AWARENESS BUILDS STRONGER ROOTS

There is a saying that goes, "The stronger roots laugh at the storm because the deeper the roots go, the higher the tree grows..." I had a neighbour who had maintained a beautiful garden with many plants that had colourful blooming flowers each day. My sister was thrilled when she saw my neighbour's garden. She decided to grow plants at her house. So, she planted one plant on her terrace, gave full attention to the plant by providing a lot of water and looked after it very well, but never observed that the water was accumulating only at the surface of the soil. One day due to heavy rains and wind, she saw the plant was damaged as it had come off from the roots. When she saw my neighbour's plant, she was perplexed as they were standing firm. She asked my neighbour despite all her good care, why couldn't the plant stand firm? My neighbour looked at the pot, smiled and said that my sister had given a lot of attention and water, but the water was accumulating only on the surface of the soil. My neighbour also added that she only poured an adequate amount of water which went deeper into the soil, making the plant stronger and there by more likely to survive the storm. During this conversation, I realised that just like the way the plant which was nurtured with lot of care (but only at the surface level of soil), which would not survive a storm, we are similar. We get anxious very easily for we are brought up in a very cozy environment. On facing a storm, when we are knocked down by any obstacle, challenges, distractions, illness, failures etc... we are shaken up. We need to water plants deeply a stronger root system as light watering tends to encourage the roots to concentrate closer to soil surface where it becomes a problem because the plants can die suddenly. In the same way, light watering which doesn't adhere during adversities, we need to water our roots such that we can resolve anything and not let the disappointments get the better of us. We must deeper our roots to build our character because the more we grow deeper the more we can grow taller and give shade to others. In the same way that we need to test the soil for amending or treating accordingly to get deeper roots, so we should not test the kind of thought we allow each day and remove the bitterness. Just like how we fertilise the soil with nutrients that are rich and organic; we need to provide heavy feeders to ourselves in the form of a good education, being disciplined, imbibing strong values and culture, being positive, building confidence and upgrading our skills to remain competitive for maximum efficiency leading to higher productivity. We can become strong through self-awareness considering our past experiences, acknowledging our strengths, staying away from vices that disturb peace, enriching our mind with good books, changing our perspective by having positive outlook and balancing emotions with logic.

## FREE YOURSELF FROM THE REPETITIVE PATTERNS OF BEHAVIOUR BY AWARENESS

Shweta is an educated, independent and bold girl, staying in a rented apartment with a plush job. Smoking makes her life except for the perpetual cough, which is her constant companion. Doctors have wanted her to stop smoking completely. She has to decide between life and smoking. She decides to quit. However, two months later she takes to smoking like fish taking to water. Her lungs started rebelling again, very badly this time. She gave a deep thought and could see smoking was really harmful. So, she gave up to give in again after a few weeks. We get angry. After sometime when we calm down, we repent because anger was not needed in that situation. We resolve not to get angry, but at first available opportunity we flare up and then after a while we repent again. Nevertheless, one is getting angry again and again despite deciding not to.

Why do we fall in these patterns again and again? It's because of lack of awareness. Be aware of your anger, love, lies and addiction. Be aware why there is anger, watch from where it is arising, how you are reacting in anger, etc.

Drop the 'H' ABIT remains.

Drop the 'A' BIT remains.

Drop the 'B' IT remains.

Only when 'I 'become aware, the 'T'-Transformation can happen.

## RAISE YOUR VIBRATION BY AWARENESS

How are you feeling right now? Good, alive, tired, run down? If something is not right you have to change it yourself. Even if you are not in mood, show compassion, show love towards people, and you will receive their good vibration, which will lift your spirit. Your vibration is a way of describing your overall state of being. "Everything in the Universe is made up of energy vibrating at different frequencies." This includes you. So, you need to be aware of how emotions are affecting you. It's also known that negative emotion lowers your frequency and positive ones raise it. Thus, the key is learning how to control our emotions rather our emotions controlling us. We can feel the vibration on an emotional level when we say that somebody is on our wavelength, or we feel in tune with a personal situation. As our inner vibration decides what kind of energies or vibrations we attract. The good thing is that if we know how to vibrate on a positive level, we can enhance our internal vibration and create a situation that reflects a more positive experience of life. How does one do it? Every day, before you go to sleep practice a mental run of all your experiences of that day. Recall and relive each one of them. Mentally, put yourself, whenever you think you were right. Analyse your mistakes and ask yourself, "What else you could have done?" Be true to yourself and honestly ask yourself, "Where all can my behaviour be improved?" This process is called introspection. Introspection helps you to look into your actions and also gain insights into your own thoughts and feelings. Introspection exercises your self-awareness and thus makes it a powerful faculty in you, instead of a dormant one. Introspection awakens your inner voice, which in turn will awaken you. You will find the motivation to do most and of what is right and also strengthen the willpower in you to reduce behaviour that you do not approve of.

## SELF-AWARENESS HELPS TRUE HAPPINESS

Consciousness is awareness of the self as the light in which thoughts, feelings and sensations shine and responses happen. The source of all conflict is the feeling we get being incomplete of being inadequate and wanting. This wanting, inadequate self, the only self of which one is aware is like the Sruti in Indian music. There is constant Sruti in our hearts which drones on: "I want this... I want that...". This constant wanting finds articulation in various specific wants, each on expression of the conclusion that one is an adequate being. What one does to achieve comfort varies from person to person. What is common is that everyone wants to acquire or get rid of something. A person desires keep changing which was once desirable may no longer be so. What never is the 'I want' Sruti in the background. The experiences of life make one think: What I want is not all these things. I want to be ease with myself. How? When the problem is identified, one knows exactly what one should look for, and life becomes purposeful. Happiness in everyday life means walking wakefully in the dream world. Self-awareness helps find true happiness.

Thus, one of the greatest blessings of being human is this gift of awareness. You alone are the only creation, who can stand apart from yourself and practice self-observation. You alone can analyse your own experiences and improve yourself. You alone can judge your own behaviour and either appreciate it or criticise it. Man alone can choose to replace some of his behavioural patterns by his own choice. And awareness entails choice. Any conscious entity is not entitled but also mandated to exercise choice every moment. Exercise of choice involves decision making. Decision making by human beings leads to performance of conscious action. The way to become conscious is to become aware. Awareness is stepping back and looking at everything for the first time. It is pulling the subjective ego state out of the equation and making an attempt to see what is way that it is. Awareness is not simple. It is something that you naturally snap into. And this is why operated disciplines like yoga, focusing on your breath, meditation, mindfulness and so on exist, and have the power to change your life for the better. And this powerful faculty of self-awareness remains dormant in most of us. By awakening it, you will start designing your own destiny. Change the content of a thief and you have a Valmiki. A sinner is transformed into a saint by transforming the content of his being. When you become the subject of your own study through Introspection, your self-judgement, your self-observation and your self-awareness will enable you to change the content of your own being. Ever since I launched into the process of transformation, it became clear to me that self-awareness itself is a scorch that would show me the way. All else was darkness. Self-awareness brought the entire contents of the subconscious mind into the conscious level greed, repressed anger, extreme inertia, indiscipline, lack of concentration, a fractured memory, indifference and various other characteristics. We can chisel ourselves into a masterpiece. Like most things in life, this simple mental tool, way too powerful. Give it a chance...

# BOOST YOUR CONFIDENCE

*"Confidence is nothing but a sense of certainity that you can do something, a belief that you will succeed in your undertakings and an absolute trust in your abilities".*

— Susan Jeffers

Are you debilitated by lack of self-confidence? Do you believe that even if you possess the skills and the required knowledge to succeed in your goals, your lack of confidence becomes a barrier to your success? Getting to grips with any set of skills requires a huge amount of work.

But you should also remember that confidence is a learned trait and not something one is born with. Even the most outwardly confident person has moments of self-doubt, when he doesn't feel at his best— but for some people, the feeling of low confidence can be an almost permanent one. Confidence is often affected by many factors — including our own feelings of self-worth or perceived degree of success or self-efficacy, the sense of competence. Given below are some of the ways to overcome confidence barrier. However, neither waving a magic band and hoping to become confident overnight nor reading them and putting them on the back burner would help. What you need to do is practice them and with time you too can become a confident person.

## ABSTAIN FROM COMPARISON

*"Don't compare yourself to others. That's when you start to lose confidence in yourself."*

— Will Smith

Comparing yourself to others is toxic. It destroys your confidence and makes you feel small. Stop comparing and start focusing on your own life. Keep moving in the direction of your goal and aspirations without worrying about what others are doing. Comparisons are unhealthy and avoided at any cost.

## **RESILIENCE**

*"Resilience is knowing that you are the only one that has the power and the responsibility to pick yourself up".*

— *Mary Holloway*

Life has a track for pulling you down several times before it takes you up to the top. Therefore, if you give up too soon you will be plagued with lack of self-confidence. But if you are a determined person who continues to fight to achieve what you deeply desire or believes in, you will experience the glow of inner confidence radiating from within you after you have reached your destination. Yet the fact remains that self-confidence is not only a destination but also a journey. Because confidence gained solely on the basis of skill and success is an incomplete one. So, humility and the readiness to learn, improve and grow are essential to building a long-time confidence in a person. Real confidence is about knowing deeply that no matter what, you will be held and supported by life. The energy of truly confident people is light, happy, positive and inclusive. And even though they may be experts in their chosen fields, they don't think they have the last word on any topic. Their eyes and ears are open to learning from others. Focus on knowing yourself and everything will fall into the place. And now you will learn that confidence really comes down to one incredibly, simple thing, which is owning it. It means that you are totally at peace with who you are in every moment, interaction and experience. You make no apologies for being awkward, nervous, excited, loud, soft spoken or something else... you are just you.

## SET REALISTIC GOALS

*"Have confidence that if you have done a little thing well, you can do a bigger thing well too."*

— *David Storey*

Having big dreams and hoping to reach the stars is wonderful. But is equally important to understand that enormous goals can undermine your confidence level. It is important to set small and realistic goals. Achieving small milestones can boost your confidence level and gradually help you achieve big dreams as well. Thus, a clear vision backed by definite plans, gives you a tremendous feeling of confidence and personal power. Set your goals high enough to inspire you and low enough to encourage you.

## SELF-LOVE, NOT SELF-CRITICISM

*"Self-compassion is a more effective motivator than self-criticism because its driving force is love, not fear"*

— *Kristen Neff*

Criticising yourself for everything, thinking, negatively about yourself, feeling you are not enough, can lead to emotional turmoil and low self-esteem. Practice self-love, honour your needs and desires and believe in yourself. Don't be critical of yourself. Be compassionate and forgiving to overcome the confidence barrier.

## FIGHT YOUR FEARS

*"The way to develop self-confidence is to do the thing you fear and get a record of successful experiences behind you".*

— *Williams Jennings Bryan*

Give up your fear of taking action. Your fear is your greatest enemy. It can steal your confidence and make you helpless. It can hinder you from achieving your goals. March ahead and strike the iron. However, not the foolish actions like jumping off a cliff on a dare. Taking action is about taking calculated risk for something you deeply feel committed or passionate about. Taking action unleashes many latent, creative, problem solving abilities within you and your confidence takes an aerial route. A fear less mind is a confident mind.

## INVEST IN YOURSELF

*"Investing in Yourself is the most important investment you'll ever make in your life."*

— *Tim Ferriss*

"Practice makes perfect" goes the popular adage. It goes without saying that the more you study your chosen subject, the more you will know about it and the more confidence you will gain. All the experts in any field are people who worked hard, practiced, disciplined themselves and gained tremendous insights in their chosen fields. No wonder their confidence levels are quite high. Go the extra mile to work on yourself. If you feel that you are not good at certain tasks, take time to master them. Consider the possible setbacks that pull you from your goals or infuse negative thoughts and work on them. Investing in yourself is another positive step towards overcoming the confidence barrier.

## GET OUT OF YOUR HEAD

*"To love yourself right now, just as you are, is to give yourself heaven.*

*Don't wait until you die.*

*If you wait, you die now, if you love, you will live now."*

— *Alan Cohen*

When you stop engaging in the present moment and begin to think about how you look, sound, feel, smell, you are creating an immediate disconnect. Whether you are disconnecting from a conversation or general experience, the effect is the same. You immediately lose confidence. This loss of confidence creates an energetic wave that is felt by everyone in the same room, interacting with you or listening you speak. It makes it harder for them to connect to your message or to you. When you catch yourself engaging in a vicious thought cycle rather than the present moment, use your senses to gently guide you back. Speak, take in the smells, notice the textures that you can feel. If you are cool and collected, then you are 100 percent engaged in the present moment.

## THINK POSITIVE

*"We become*

*what*

*We think about"*

— *Emily Nightingale*

If you are constantly nurturing the negative thoughts, you will slowly become what you are preaching inside your head. It is very important to take control of your thoughts. Whenever your mind is surrounded by negative ideas, switch them to positive thoughts. This will enhance your confidence and build your emotional as well as mental health. So, coach yourself to think in a positive manner. The more your energies clear up, the more your confidence will shoot up. Let go of your victim-hood. It traps you in a vibrational mode and nibbles away confidence.

## TRUST YOUR INSTINCTS

*"Have the confidence to trust your gut feeling and choose your moment to act. Timing is everything".*

— *LuLu Guinness*

Once you have done this, pay attention to the gut feeling. You will be surprised at the good advice your subconscious can give when you listen to it. Your instinct is the knowing that arises from your gut. It is knowing within yourself which never goes wrong and can safely be trusted. Act upon it without fear or hesitation. With constant repetition, affirmations telling that all is well will help you drown out the negative messages of your subconscious mind. "Even if things are not going the way you want them to go, you simply trust that all things happen for a reason and decide you will learn and grow from it." As you become more powerful and loving, you draw healthier people into your life."

## OWN IT, WHATEVER IT IS

*"Self-confidence Is the*

*Best outfit, Rock it*

*And own it"*

— *Nohin*

Last but not the least, you should create an instant and unshakable confidence is to totally own it. Whether it is your opinion, emotions, feeling, words or choice of dessert, just own it. Don't give a single thought to what anyone else would think of what you are doing. You are you, you want what you want and you do what you do.

If you are feeling sad or moody, just own it. Be sad, be moody. Are you nervous? Own it. Tell everyone that you are nervous. This stops the process of entering your head dead in its tracks. Being totally okay with whatever emotions sensations or feelings you are experiencing in any given moment results in the appearance of total confidence.

Only stubborn self-confidence can steer your ship towards the oceans of victory, or else your vessel would always be docked at the harbour. Never think it's too late. The right time is now. Gather your courage and set sail for wonderful climes. It need not be a long journey; even a short jaunt will rejuvenate and exhilarate you greatly. Happy sailing!

# BUILD YOUR SELF-ESTEEM

*"Self-esteem comes from being able to define the world in your own terms and refusing to abide by the judgements of others".*

— *Oprah Winfrey*

Self-esteem is a major element which can determine success and failure and it is a demon all of us battle with at some point in our life. Most people think of it as a nightmare or probably get depressed or indulge in self-pity. However, all inner work begins with developing sound self-esteem. Without self-esteem, it is virtually impossible to look within and contain what we see. Even we cannot interact with people on equal basis. We will not be able to establish boundaries and we will look so strongly for the love, appreciation and endorsement we should get from our self, in others that we will give away all our power to them.

## STEPS FOR BUILDING POSITIVE SELF-ESTEEM

*"Most fears of rejection rest on the desire for approval from other people. Don't bare your self-esteem on their opinions."*

— *Harvey Mackay*

1. Turn negative scars into positive stars, adversity into advantage and stumbling blocks into stepping stones.
2. Let your imagination run beyond academic limitations. Don't let education put limitations on you.
3. Be a volunteer. The process of giving without having expectations or getting anything in return raises one's self-esteem.
4. Accept responsibility for one's behaviour, actions, and insulate oneself from excuses.
5. Practice self-discipline.

6. Set realistic goals.
7. Associate with people of high moral character.
8. Become internally driven, not externally driven.
9. Develop a mind-set that brings happiness.
10. Learn to find pleasure in every little thing.
11. Be honest yourself.
12. Forgive yourself and others. Don't hold guilt or bear grudges.

## ADVANTAGES OF HAVING HIGH SELF-ESTEEM

Builds strong confidence. Always willing to accept duties and tasks. Builds optimistic attitudes, develops a caring attitude and makes a person sensitive to others needs.

Instils self-motivation, ambition and makes one more sensitive. Make a person ready to face new opportunities and challenges. Improves the performance in different fields and increases risk taking ability. Helps a person in giving and receiving both criticism and compliments, easily and with ease.

*"Low self-esteem is like driving through life with your hand break on."*
— Maxwell Maltz

## HOW TO RECOGNISE LOW SELF-ESTEEM

Low self-esteem makes you vulnerable to manipulation and therefore you will operate from positions of weakness and helplessness.

1. Lack of confidence
2. Having negative expectations of yourself and seldom disappointed by those expectations.

3. Lack of assertiveness.
4. Exhibition of attention seeking activities.
5. Indecisive and running away from responsibility. Lack of courage and fear of criticism leading to indecisive behaviour.
6. Feeling unworthy. More emphasis given to net worth than self-worth.

## HEAL YOUR SELF-ESTEEM

One reason why a common man has difficulty in believing that he deserves or can achieve what he wants to is that his self-esteem is usually damaged. The good news is that it can be revived. The baby elephant is tied with a strong steel chain, which it ceaselessly attempts to break away from but fails. The result? The elephant owner doesn't need to use metallic chain to tie it any longer when it grows to a powerful adult. Why? Because as a result of the thousands of unsuccessful attempts it made as an infant, the elephant developed an unshakable conviction about its inability to break away from whatever it is tied. Unfortunately, parents and teachers, though only unknowingly, let a similar process run through our own children as well. Their ability to dream has been forfeited by the society. And since he cannot dream, he doesn't feel challenged. In the absence of challenges, he cannot feel the need to mobilise his dormant inner resources. In reply to a teacher's advice, "Hard work never kills", a student replied: "But why take a chance?" Thus, we like this student ask ourselves: "Why try, when I am not sure that it will".

In short self-esteem is the composite of two things. One is self-efficacy or the ability to trust one's effectiveness and competence in coping with life. The other is self-worth or the knowledge that one is worthy of life, love and all the good things in life. Most of us have dents and fissures dealt on our ego in the process of living. It is this that makes us of insecure and ensure of ourselves. A sound ego is the result of sound self-esteem. Among the characteristics of a sound ego would be the ability to draw boundaries between ourselves and others so no one can dominate or control you, to be open to life, to take risks, to be assertive, to take the failures and disappointments of life without losing the faith in oneself or life. High self-esteem leads to a happy gratifying and purposeful life. So, let's create a better world by creating better relationships. There doesn't seem to be any other way. Each and every one of us has self-esteem within us to be an inspiring individual.

## BE YOUR OWN BEST FRIEND

You are with YOU every year, every day, every hour and every second. I did not say like your good points and bad points. I said like YOU. Like yourself. Soon you will relax and start looking at the things you do not like, changing what you can and accepting what you cannot. That is when the miracle occurs. When you like yourself, you go beyond the barriers of loneliness. Your appearance changes, even if you do nothing to make it look different on the outside. People will be drawn to you. Your boss, your friends... Everyone will recognize your talents. This is because when you do so, you have a vibration of being content. You will be happy. When you are happy, it just reflects in your face. Having yourself as a best friend has advantages.

**SWIRLING THOUGHTS**

Almost everyone is prone to negative thinking, at least once in a while. As dark thoughts whirl around in our heads, our problems balloon out of proportion. We may berate ourselves, curse our bad luck and feel miserable about our fate. Likewise, I suck at Chemistry. I am the only one who hasn't landed an internship. I will never be able to crack the CAT. All my close are dating someone. Why am I the only Singleton? My parents don't understand me. I'll never amount to anything in my life. Why me? However, if a friend had come to us with similar problems, chances are that we would have given them uplifting advice. We may have helped reframe their negative thoughts to that they felt better about their problems and themselves. So, when you are feeling low and don't have anyone to turn to, just pause and listen to the thoughts that swirl through your mind. You may have failed a test, botched up a job interview or broken up with a romantic partner.

Instead of simply giving into the black thoughts and feelings that cloud your mind, pause and listen to your internal commentary. Thoughts that simply pop up in our heads are referred to as "automatic thoughts". If your automatic thoughts are making you feel miserable, don't succumb to them, as we are won't to do. Instead listen to them like an outsider. In fact, writing down may be useful. You are not here by coincidence. Go beyond and see how being YOU, can change your life and others.

## START LIKING YOURSELF

A year ago, I met a beautiful lady. Her husband had been cheating on her and she wanted some advice regarding her future. Even though her eyes were dull, shoulders drawn and her face sad, I managed to look beyond that, look beyond her sadness. Did you know that when you go "beyond", you can create new things? I told her to go look in my bathroom mirror. She came back and asked her what she saw. "A fool" she replied. I told her that she needed glasses and to go and look again. And again. By the third time she was almost in tears but she managed to acknowledge that she was beautiful. When we are in extreme trauma, the spirit cracks, even fractures into tiny pieces. In order to put that together, you need to start fitting piece by piece. No one in this world can make you happy. You need to like yourself and achieve happiness from within. Nothing can bring happiness in you except you. Your lover or your husband or your parents can add that happiness. Our happiness is based on conditions. I will be happy if and then follows the, if I win a million, if my husband is less grumpy, if I meet a lover. Not so. Happiness is the emotion that produces tingly sensation in the brain. That is why chocolate uplifts the spirit. The brain sees this as happy food and soon you feel better!

In order to really like yourself, you need to embrace your good points and divide your bad points into two groups. There is a group of bad points that you cannot change and the one you cannot. If you are five feet and two inches tall and you don't like it, so sorry, you have to deal with that. No miracle can turn you into a six-footer. There are lots of things in life that you cannot change. In order to be happy, you need to accept them and learn to live with it. Change what you can and look at what you cannot change from a different angle. Did you realise that being short has its own advantages? Look beyond the physical, emotional and mentally self. See the perfection of your spirit is allowed to shine through your emotions and thoughts. It will lighten you and you will feel happy. Nothing is impossible. 'Nothing 'does not exist. Therefore, you need to accept that all things are possible. No one is just good or bad. If you don't have bad points, there is imbalance, because the YOU as focal point needs good and bad in order to show balance. Even the most successful people have weaknesses. That beautiful young woman did all these things. Soon, her eyes sparkled and she was even lovelier than before. Her shimmering spirit and kind nature drew lots of friends to her. At one stage she even had a choice of men wanting to be with her all the time! But she chose one. She shares her secret of inner and outer beauty. She is her own best friend and she really likes herself. Be you. Like who you are. Trust yourself and have faith in the Creator. You have to be happy for yourself. If you find that hard, look for someone to help you achieve that. Enjoy discovering your inner beauty. When you like yourself, you go beyond the barriers of loneliness.

Chapter 03
# CULTIVATE CONSISTENCY

# CULTIVATE CONSISTENCY

*"Consistency is the key to achieving and maintaining momentum".*

*—Darren Hardy*

Being consistent is one of the most important factors that lead to success, but most of us find it hard to maintain the drive. Consistency is important on a personal level. Since loving yourself is a process, allow yourself to make some concrete goals on how to accomplish this. Develop some long-range plans for going towards what might inspire you. It may be what you do in your work or something new you want to learn. Much like a rope that leaves a dent on the parapet of a well by consistently grazing the same spot every time, one can acquire any skill by practicing it regularly. In the age of instant gratification, this mantra seems oddly out of place, or more like out of ethos. And yet, this is what eventually leads to one's evolution.

## SIGNIFICANCE OF CONSISTENCY

*"Do it again and again. Consistency makes the rain drops to create holes in the rock. Whatever is difficult can be done easily with regular attendance, attention and action".*

*— Israel more Ayivor*

Consistency is a fundamental aspect of effective action. Success is not that momentous action you take today or some other day, nor is it a stroke of luck, or magical quantum leap that you will take to make a difference. Nothing great was ever achieved by those who apply themselves 'once a while'. Prosperity or abundance may begin with a mindset, but they are not achieved in that moment. Although it is important to dream and visualise abundance to send clear signals to your mind, mere visualisation does not discount the hard work you have to put in, that too regularly, to manifest that abundance and make it your reality. Abundance is found consistently putting one step after the other. Whatever you do consistently every day decides your direction in life. It is that simple and that which creates the monumental difference between where you are now and where you will be in a handful of days. Thus, consistency is self-discipline in action.

## TIME AND CONSISTENCY

*"A little time and consistency can build a great foundation for something with meaning."*

— *Lisa Yurkiw Bitton*

To be consistent means to fully dedicate yourself completely to a task, activity, or goal. It means to stay engaged without distraction, day after day. Time plays a significant role in this whole concept of consistency. One can be extremely motivated and enthusiastic about achieving one's goal, but what happens when they do not get the desired results? That is the time when a person's strength of character gets tested.

Most of us must have heard about former president of India, late Dr. APJ Abdul Kalam's inspirational journey from his humble roots to the Rashtrapati Bhavan, the most prestigious building in the nation. When Dr Kalam's first major project as a scientist, SL V3 failed for the first time in 1979, he was shattered. This project was the culmination of 10 years of hard work of numerous researchers and scientists. Around the time, Dr Kalam's childhood friend, Jalaluddin — to whom he was deeply attached — passed away. And yet, he did not think of quitting the project. He said, *"I knew that for [achieving] success, we have to work hard and need perseverance".* 11 months later, the team successfully launched SL V3 in their second attempt under the leadership of the brilliant Dr Kalam. *"There is no greater power in heaven or on earth than commitment to a dream."* said the incredible Dr. Kalam.

## CONSISTENCY IMPOSES COMMITMENT

*"Never Give Up!*

*"Without Commitment, you will*

*never start:*

*Without Consistency, you will*

*never finish."*

—Denzel Washington

To be consistent requires commitment on your part. It requires that you commit yourself to sustained effort over the long term. What this essentially means is that you keep your word to yourself and others that you will follow through with what you set out to do consistently over a period of time, up until the moment your objectives are achieved. As such, consistency is all about your ability to be dependable, reliable, and responsible for all your choices, decisions, and actions. Take daily steps to refine who you are in an effort to be ready for all decisions that need integrity and forethought. When you are self-respecting, you make the commitment to be at the top of your game. You refuse to live by the "I will do it later motto." You get things done today to ensure a successful tomorrow. Regular and persistent efforts determine your ability to be a reliable and trusted decision maker.

## WHY IS IT DIFFICULT TO BE CONSISTENT?

*"It's not what we do once in a while that shapes our lives. It's what we do consistently"*

— *Anthony Robbins*

What usually happens is that we combust all our energy and enthusiasm in the initial days of walking the path that leads to our goal. We overdose on practice and overwhelm ourselves with motivational paraphernalia. Much like the over-enthusiastic athlete who spends all his energy in gaining the lead in the first lap of the relay race but eventually burns out and loses, we also lose sight of the long path lying ahead of us in order to maintain the lead. Or, in some cases, we are unable to put a lid on our enthusiasm and channel it in a fruitful manner. A far better approach is that of a tortoise. Each step may seem to take forever, but no matter how uninspired you feel, continue to follow your practice schedule precisely and consistently. This is how we can use our greatest enemy, habit, against the habit of consistency isn't about obtaining quick results. It is rather about making incremental progress and improvements over an extended period of time. However, if it looks like a big deal to inculcate the habit of being consistent, recall all those poor habits that you have adopted mindlessly.

## HOW TO BE CONSISTENT?

*"When you look at people who are successful, you will find that they aren't the people who are motivated, but have consistency in their motivation"*

— *Arsene Wenger*

1. Repeating something over and over again forms the foundation of any skill we want to learn. However, being consistent makes different demands on different individuals. "Consistency-in-action" is about learning, growing and adapting your actions that can help you lead to incremental improvements over an extended period of time. Following are a practical steps that help you become consistent:
2. Develop focus: When you consistently focus on the smaller steps on a daily, weekly, and monthly basis and execute them one by one, it will certainly lead to the bigger picture.
3. Develop winning habits: Success is often a result of certain habits practiced on a regular basis. For instance, if you want to drop four inches from your waist in next two months, you need to develop specific habits— a strict diet, exercise routine, positive affirmations— which need consistent practice. When you embrace these habits as winning habits, the sense of joy and achievement you feel each day acts as a silent motivator for you to help you go further till you achieve your goal.
4. Tackle boredom: Feeling bored does not kill consistency. To do away with the monotony of a routine, bring some variety to it. Focus on how best you can enjoy the routine itself. Apply it to various areas in your life too. For instance, I include small 'outside of work' activities in my routine to keep boredom away, like doing some art and craft, watering plants, preparing a new dish, or reading a different blog. I vary their schedule every day to do away with monotony.
5. Use your environment: Your environment is full of triggers that cause emotional responses on the conscious and

unconscious level. Use it to your advantage and make your environment a constant reminder of things you need to do, have to do, and will do.

6. The journey of life is all about betterment and self-growth, and it yields its results only to those who are willing to put in all that it takes to achieve their goals. Consistency and indefatigable efforts are one of those key elements. To be consistent means understanding that the greatest power lies in the present moment. Therefore, consistency demands that you stay vigilant, mindful, and present for the task at hand, without losing focus. It demands that you are able to discipline yourself for this moment — and only to this moment — without exception.

## Chapter 04
# DISCOVER YOURSELF
# DEFINE YOURSELF
# DATE WITH YOURSELF

# DISCOVER YOURSELF

*"The definition of insanity is doing the same thing over and over again and expecting different results."*

— *Albert Einstein*

We all come to this world to experience our own reality - to learn who we are by being what we thought would be best for us. Eventually, most of us reach a place where we are not so content with doing our lives in the old ways. Most people may never recognise this state when it happens. They may go on doing life as they always have until they die discontented. This is not the way life was intended to be lived here. But it is the way many people live. Life is intended to be lived here in great joy, with great wisdom, and with energy abounding. Why then so many people live in a state of fear or confusion or exhaustion or depression? I believe it's often because they are not living the true life, they came to live and their mind and body know it. They know it on such a deep level that can't keep themselves from feeling discomfort and discontentment.

## A GOAT'S LIFE

It was a chilly November morning. All four limbs tied up together and fixed precariously on to the back of a moped, the two black goats showed no resistance... They did not seem to comprehend their impending fate, yet they looked around at the roadside trees, shops, the passing traffic and finally turning towards us, they looked into my eyes with that same vacant stare. As I was returning home from market on scooter along with my husband, travelling the same road and following the moped that carried those goats hurriedly to the butcher shop, their destination. A deep sigh surged from the pit of my stomach instantly choking my throat. A realisation hit me that their plight was nothing but being controlled by fate; they lacked any purpose on their own, except for being bred, fed, and cared for only for their flesh and skin.

Yes, being human, we are innately blessed with the capacity to think. We can continue to exist and at the same time we can question our existence as we understand that there is something called 'existence '. Yet most of us end up never having to figure out what life means to us. When given the greatest choice of discovering one's life, are we merely wasting it living the goat's life? A life lived without questioning its purpose and then trying to live up to that without making it meaningful to its truest sense, is an ultimate disrespect to our existence.

## MEANING OF SELF-DISCOVERY

*"An unquestioned mind is the world of suffering."*

— *Byron Katie*

I know that for me there were many years in which I sensed that I wasn't doing my life exactly as I needed. I was either in the wrong profession, living in the wrong place, or with the wrong people, or trying to convince myself that I was happy. It wasn't working. I knew in my heart that I didn't have time to continue living that way, that if I did; I would never be happy or fulfill my life's purpose. Today I have reached a place where I feel relatively content with my life, though many people living in the old ways might be prone to wonder. I am living so far outside the box of typical human existence that I imagine. I make no sense to them. Because now I see my life as a joyous walk through a beautiful land, encumbered only by my own ability to express joy and give and receive love. If I learn to do these things to the best of my ability, then there is no more for me to do here — ever. I exist here only to discover the parts of me which have been dormant, waiting for the right moment to come forward. This is what is meant by self - discovery— finding the parts which need to come forward and allowing them to express through us in whatever way seems most appropriate.

When we first come here, I believe many of us don't know how to relax and be ourselves. We may be following someone else's mandates and beliefs, or we may be allowing ourselves to remain blocked until we are ready to fully experience our truth. Do you see what I mean? Have you found your life blocked or unrewarding? Can you see new ways in which you may enjoy your life, if you gave yourself the chance? Look deeper inside yourself and discover where your joy may lie dormant. Look until you find the things which bring you joy and then begin doing them. You may not find your truth entirely the next moment.

It usually take years for one to open fully to one's self, after years of self-denial. But you can begin to discover the things, which have always bought you joy and allow yourself, to begin doing them. This is a time to be who we are. It's a time to allow that to be enough. It's not a time to seek ourselves in the external world, for that world holds no answers for us. Our truths are within us, deep inside where we place them for later discovery. Many of us are now at the place where we have no alternative but to be true to ourselves. This is the way we planned it when we came here. If you are like me, you have found that you can no longer pretend that the old ways are serving you. You know you must go forward into a new reality which may be unknown and may be more than a little bit frightening. We are often afraid to move into the Light, to be someplace we may know is real but we can't quite remember. One must move into the light in baby steps until one is ready to run with it. But holding back from it entirely brings great pain. The pain you feel in your soul may be from holding yourself back from experiencing joy and love.

How to find oneself? Look inside where the answers are buried. Be who you are to be the best of your ability each moment. Allow yourself to experience your reality as fully as possible, as if you then discover there are places which are not in alignment with your truth, allow them to slowly dissolve, to release from your being. As you become more aligned with your truth, you become happier with your life— even though you are letting of many aspects of your former self. Your life comes more into balance; you become the being you came here to be.

## DISCOVER YOURSELF THROUGH WORK

Hold the sanctity of work above everything, and everything else will flow into your life as by-products. From the food we eat to the clothes we wear to the roof above our head to the comforts we enjoy to whatever we are able to materialistically give to our loved ones... everything is from the earnings we get out of our work. From our identity to the dignity with which we live our life are all rewards from the work we do. Work expands your personality. Align yourself to the old-time adage: 'Work is worship'. Your work hours, compensation, position are all mere details compared to your inner potential manifesting through your work. Work serves your evolution like nothing else can. Go the extra mile... deliver more than what is expected of you. Give your very best and strive to be the best in whatever you do. Let your heart beat in gratitude for your work. Carry respect for your work place. Focus on 'How you work' and not 'How much you work'. Go to work with the same reverence and devotion as you would have for a place of worship. Expect more from yourself than what others expect of you. Align yourself to the highest work ethics. Continuously keep upgrading your competence levels.

It is a true story that Dave Anderson and Jim Murphy joined American Railways on the same day. Twenty years later, Dave was still doing the same job, but Jim became the Chairman of the Railways. Dave said, *"I came to work for $1.75 an hour; Jim came to work for American Railways. That made all the difference".*

Work is our only salvation. Work is the only way to progress. Nothing develops man like work does. When any work is done as a choice, you tend to enjoy what you do, and when it is finally completed, you experience a sense of fulfilment. That which gives you fulfilment you look forward to doing it again and again and again... On the contrary, when any work is undertaken as a compulsion, you tend to struggle doing what you do, and when it is finally completed, you experience only a sense of relief. That which gives you relief, you just want to avoid it in the future. Even if you do it again, you will only do it reluctantly. If everything essential about work is seen as a compulsion, if everything is pursued as struggle and if everything is completed with a sigh of relief... How can we improve the quality of our work in life? Please! shift from the attitude of "I must do. I should do." to "I WANT to do". Let work become a form of celebration for you. Whistle your way to work and dance your way back home. Thus, work must be the primary form of worship. What you get by achieving your goal is insignificant compared to what you become in achieving your goal. It is not about awards, rewards or satisfaction. They are mere by products for a man who discovers himself through work.

Happiness is the by-product of doing work that gives you inner expression. Success is the by-product of the world recognising the value you add through your work. And when your work and results of your work becomes useful to the world, the by-product is that you discover the purpose of your life.

# DEFINE YOURSELF

*"Accept no one's definition of your life, define yourself"*

— *Robert Frost*

The only person who decides how you define yourself is you. Never be bullied into silence. Never allow yourself to be made into a victim. You are not defined by what happens to you but by the choices you make. You have to fall in love with yourself before anyone will fall in love with you.

## WHO DEFINES YOUR LIFE?

*"You can't define yourself by other people's limited Expectations"*

— *Michelle Obama*

Nancy, a young brilliant executive in her mid-thirties, shared her state of grief in one of her counselling sessions with me. "I have a knotted pain in my heart... it is full of tears and now it has turned into ice. But I will get over this trying phase soon". Disowned and rejected several times by her husband, when she loved, trusted and still does, Nancy is a calm, heroic figure that believes in herself and in God. Although she weeps uncontrollably and unabashedly, her grief has not left her bitter, cynical or resentful. Instead she is a stronger and gentler human being, closer to herself and to the suffering of humanity. Interestingly, Nancy's husband did return to her, only because she dared to endure, understand and believe in their love, which, in case, has been masked by fears and phobias. Nancy's case is just one example of people who go through various kinds of life crisis and come out rich in soul and spirit instead of broken in body and heart. Her example site so many lessons to learn and live: share what you are going through with the people who are related to or affected by the situation. We should do what we need to and want to do in life, conforming to what is 'right'. We need to draw a boundary around ourselves from the comments of others. We need to be compassionate and yet confront others, if needed. We need to define our life in the way WE need to live it.

## REFRAME THE SITUATION

It's not what you go through that defines you; you can't help that. It's what you do after you have gone through it that really tests who you are. Some people are naturally good at thinking positively or looking for the value of any situation. These are the types of people who get tough during tough times and have an optimistic attitude. They have the capability of reframing the whole situation in a very unique manner. Reframing is the ability to look at a situation or circumstance in a new way giving it a more positive or insightful spin. We have to stop being afraid of what can go wrong and start being positive about what can go right. The most successful people are ones who stayed strong against all odds.

What happens in life does not define us. What defines us is how we progress forward, how we take life head on, how we grow and continue to live. When we reframe a critical situation, it gives us the energy to carry on even when the chips are down. Let's develop this essential art of reframing tough situations and turn the moment of grief into a moment of celebration! Be that pillar of strength to define yourself.

## HOW TO DEFINE YOURSELF?

*" Trying to define yourself is like trying to bite your own teeth"*

— *Alan Watts*

Be careful how you characterise yourself. Don't characterise or define yourself by some temporary quality. We can choose any characteristic to define us. But we need to know that when we choose to define ourselves or to present ourselves by some characteristic that is temporary or trivial in eternal terms, we de-emphasise what is most important about us and we over-emphasise what is relatively unimportant. This can lead us down the wrong path and hinder our future progress.

For example, a person who calls himself "underachiever" tends to look for - or encourage others to look for - things that interpret his behaviour in those terms. That has a very different consequence than if he and others looked on his quality of 'underachieving' as simply a temporary tendency that needed to be disciplined, in the course of seeking graduation, employment or life itself. Stop looking for magic. You are it! Always redefine in a positive way. Action follows definition, so if you define yourself as a runner, you will become one. If you define yourself as honest, you will work to be more honest. Stop letting your old definitions limit who or what you can become. Tell yourself and tell the world what your life is about. Not by talking the talk, but by defining it. Mahatma Gandhi once said, *"My life is my message."* What kind of message do you want to leave behind?

# DATE WITH THE SELF

*"Loneliness is the poverty of self, solitude is the richness of self"*

— May Sarton

Solitude is the joyful experience of one's own self. It is the ability to spend time with our self in a state of completion and plenitude. When we are truly attuned with ourselves, we need no one or nothing else. In the most essential way therefore, the ability to be with ourselves is testimony of our completion of a journey. It begins with the normal physical, emotional and psychological needs of human condition. We look for love, for appreciation, for acknowledgment and understanding. We look for physical companionship and affection, and for security. We look for guidance and support, for someone to show us the way. We look for all these things outside ourselves. It is only when something shifts and we start locating the source of these things within us the journey starts. Gradually, we crest these needs as we begin to increasingly experience inner love, inner security, inner strength. And with each turn of the screw, our friendship with ourselves deepens and we feel replete within ourselves, whole, perfect and complete.

## GIFTS OF SOLITUDE

The gifts of solitude are precious and many-layered, beginning with developmental needs and going all the way to the ultimate state of becoming. You are watching, observing, and examining what happens in the absence of the process of becoming.....The observation does not imply giving in or surrendering; it implies a non-reactionary attentiveness. Meaningful aloneness gifts us heightened sensitivity to our breath, and then that focus and sensitivity is transferred to sights, sounds, sensations, thoughts, intentions, and emotions. Some time alone is essential for developing cognitive skills, which is something beyond memory. For it is only when we are alone, we assimilate our own feelings and experiences.

## HEALING

Most of us don't want to be alone for any period of time—and certainly not when there is a crisis, but perhaps that's exactly what we need to do. Advice, counselling and time with others can be helpful, but only to a point. Ultimately the acceptance, wisdom and understanding that we seek is within us. Dr. Ken Weizer was a Hollywood filmmaker when he was diagnosed with cancer, he took a nine-month sabbatical from his work. He was going through tremendous emotional and spiritual upheaval. Moving to a tiny town outside San Francisco, he spent time primarily with himself, taking long hikes all alone. *"This solitude became the space to heal"* he says.

*"Before cancer I had seen life as a linear, and I feared the end of the line. But as I hiked more and more, my screaming mind began to quieten down, and I started to see the miracle of death all around me and... the seed of rebirth was sown in the soil of my death."* Taking a cue from his learning, he took the radical step of leaving his Hollywood career to learn naturopathy and has since, become a naturopathy doctor, in a 'rebirth' of sorts. It was solitude that helped him immensely to connect within. *"Within solitude I have found connection to self, my own feelings and needs, connection to others, and empathy for the world"* he says, affirming that solitude which is *"self-care, self-awareness and self-love is essential for a fulfilled life".*

## BONDING WITH NATURE

Only in solitude can we truly experience nature and avail of its teachings. Every one knows the sensation of seeing a wonderful sunset, watching the endless dance of sea waves, or looking down a view from the top of a steep mountain. We find ourselves so uplifting in awe that we are 'speechless '— an apt word for the sublime feeling that nature creates in us. Bonding with nature is the easiest and most effective feel-good therapy; nature accepts and therefore affirms our faith in ourselves. Henry David Thoreau, the author of Walden, an autobiographical account of his experiment in solitary living, writes, *"Sometimes, in a summer morning, having taken my accustomed bath, I sat in my sunny doorway from sunrise till noon, rapt in a revelry, amidst the pines and hickories and sumaches, in undisturbed solitude and stillness, while the birds sing around or flitted noiseless through the house, until by the sun falling in at my west window, or the noise of some traveller's wagon on the distant highway, I was reminded of the lapse of time. I grew in those seasons like corn in the night, and they were far better than any work of the hands would have been. They were not time subtracted from my life, but so much over and above my usual allowance."*

## FOSTERING CREATIVITY

Today, sights and sounds of technology and media permeate both public and private spaces, making it difficult to find quiet places for reflection and thoughts. But it is essential that we do so. In silence, we often say, we can hear ourselves think; but perhaps it is more appropriate to say that in silence we can hear ourselves not think and hence, we go into a place far deeper than we ever thought existed. It is from silence that all acts of creation are born

— works of art, music, writing, and even scientific inventions. All artist, thinkers and philosophers, have actively sought solitude.

Thoreau writes, *"I love to be alone. I never found the companion that was so companionable as solitude".* In fact, it was when realisation of his growing deafness that spelt doom for his career as a concert pianist, forced him to increasingly find solace in his own company, that musical genius, Ludwig Van Beethoven's creative forces at a composer were fully unleashed. Withdrawing into a deeply private world of his own, he gave the world music of unprecedented intensity and originality that many believe would not have been possible, but for his deafness and the near-monastic withdrawal from society that it imposed on him.

## A KEY TO SPIRITUALITY

It is in silence that we are able to hear the voice of God, expressed to us in a myriad way. *"A man who loves God, necessarily loves silence,"* wrote Thomas Merton, a prolific writer, Trappist monk and connoisseur of silence. Surely, it is no coincidence that places of worship are places of silence — nurturing and enhancing the spiritual quest. *"In the Kathopanishad, it is said that the mind is like a charioteer who needs to remain calm to rein the wild horses, which are our senses. It is to develop this inner calm that we need to cultivate solitude."*, says Swami Tanmayananda, from the Ramkrishna Mission, Malaysia. Psychologists say that during silence, the mind is best able to cultivate a form of mindful intention that motivates us to take action. At that point we have to ask ourselves three questions.

- If anything were possible, what would I welcome or create in my life?

- When I am feeling most courageous and inspired, what do I want to offer the world?
- When I'm honest about how I suffer, what do I want to make peace with?

In short solitude — a boon to the introspective mind, to the creative spirit and to the seeker. That is why we need to recognise and harness the power of solitude. Taking first step in connecting to ourselves, we will realise and recognise our unique potential and move closer to the realisation that we are complete in ourselves and also a part of vast cosmos.

Chapter 05
# EMBRACE YOURSELF EMBRACE YOUR FLAWS

## EMBRACE YOURSELF

*"When we express our true self, we become comfortable in our skin. The self- berating diminishes and we worry less about the future. We are comfortable in the present, and do not carry the past with us"*

— *LOUISE HAY*

The search for our authentic identity is a long and changing journey. As human beings, we are programmed to evolve. Who you are today is not who you were yesterday, or who you will be tomorrow! Change is scary. Embrace it. Change is usually not a question of self-motivation. Often, we have a tough time getting ourselves to change because we have mixed emotions about change and are unsure of what is store for us if we change. Unknown pleasure does not overpower known pain. People prefer to go through practiced pain because they are used to it, rather than investing time to go through the change. We must realise the fact that with every change that we go through, we become a better person. Pre-change and post-change are always comfortable, but the transition period is never comfortable. It is not a question of delaying or avoiding change, but a matter of managing the transition positively. The key is to get strong reasons as to why change must take place immediately and not someday in the future. If you are not driven to make the change now, then you may never make the change ever. To expedite change, we must see ourselves as the only source of change. Otherwise we will always be looking for someone else to make the changes for us and we will always have someone else to blame when it doesn't work. Remember," Things don't change; we change."

A gentle evening breeze caressed her cheeks as Suman sat on the balcony of her eight-floor apartment overlooking the Arabian Sea. She relished this time of the day the most; the time when she has the house all to herself. Her son, Rachit, was at his swimming practice and her husband, Manoj, was at the gym. The breathtaking sunset, the cool sea breeze, and a cup of masala tea were all she had for company. But today, the tea seemed extra special though. She was now a manager at a multinational company who loved her job and her life. She often sat in the mellow glow of the sunset, her heart brimming with gratitude. As she watched the foamy waves lash against the shore and recede back into the sea, her thoughts retreated to the day it all began, 10 years ago. Looking back Suman twitched nervously as she sat outside the principal's office, in her son's school, waiting to be summoned. She held a crumpled piece of paper bearing the marks of being read multiple times. She had pored over the words repeatedly while trying to fathom why it had been addressed specifically to her. It had clearly stated that only she as a parent be present to meet the principal. "What has Rachit done wrong?"- She wondered or was it her? Had she not been a good mother? Before she could come up with another plausible reason, the principal, Mrs. Dezousa beckoned Suman to her cabin. After exchanging pleasantries the principal got straight to the point. Several times she noticed Rachit sitting all by himself while the other kids played. On being questioned, he told her that he was upset because he had seen his mother cry every night and was taking the blame on himself for not being a good boy. 'I do not mean to intrude but it breaks my heart to see a six-year-old child affected by his mother's emotions. Is there any way we can help?'

Ms Dezuosa asked gently. The genuine concern in her voice brought tears to Suman's eyes. "I...don't know what to do?

Nothing I do is ever right," she said in between sniffles. Nothing I make is good enough for mother-in-law. If Rachit does not eat, she says I don't know how to feed him. If he watches TV, she says I am spoiling him, yet she lets him watch all those dreadful TV serials she's addicted to. If I make him study, she says I am pushing him and so on it goes. I never seem to do anything right. And Manoj is always busy in his corporate life'. Her sniffles had turned into a full-blown rant, rocked with sobs. 'My dear you need to get a few facts straight', said Ms Desuoza continuing, 'You cannot live your life according to someone else's expectation for you. If you do, you will always fall short and spend the rest of your life trying to fulfil expectations that come attached to various roles assigned to you. And in this process, you are bound to lose yourself. Your mother-in-law is old and with age comes rigidity. Accept it and move on. Trying to be a perfect daughter-in-law is like trying to reach for the pot of gold at the other end of rainbow, 'the principal explained. 'And you are not helping your child by staying home and being miserable', she added. 'It's very important to take out time for yourself every day and do something you enjoy. Did you have a hobby growing up? asked the principal. May be dancing or music? Embroidery? The emptiness in Suman's gaze was suggestive of a spirit dulled, lost in the maze of life. Silence ensued. Finally, she spoke, "I used to enjoy painting as a child". "There you go. Just take a few minutes every day to paint. For those few minutes let it be just you and the canvas. Take baby steps my dear, and see how things change." The turn of events since then had only be pleasant. She took her advice seriously. Every afternoon, she would pour her pent-up emotions on the canvas, and the results were brilliant jewels of art. In no time Suman was designing and painting beautiful works of art for a designer boutique. She also joined a part-time Master's in management course. One thing led to another and brought Suman to where she is today. She was now a manager at a multinational company who loved her job and her life. The intimacy towards her true self extended and she enveloped the whole family into a blanket of love.

"Embrace Yourself" is not some tangible thing to do. You don't have to like everything. You don't have to "condone" it. To embrace yourself, you have to STOP doing something what we humans do way too much; negative self judgement. It is damaging emotionally and it leads to all sorts of problems. As well as damaging your self-esteem can be associated with anxiety or depression. It may prevent you from doing things you want and it can isolate you from people. Stopping the negative self judgement is all about changing your thoughts and words. Stop putting yourself down. Practice being present and noticing things as they are without making a judgement. Don't judge yourself negatively based on a single experience. Instead focus on the lessons you've learned, what you did well, and think of failure as a growth opportunity. The more you talk or think about yourself in a negative way, the more you believe it. Get out of that habit. Know that you are not stupid, ugly or incompetent even if you believe it. Accept compliments with gratitude. It's important to know that change is not going to happen overnight. Stopping the negative self-judgement will take effort and commitment on your part. Do something that you are good at every day. Be it writing, singing or dancing. Contribute your value to the world. You will embrace yourself if your interests and talents are not self-centred. You have to think something that is larger than yourself and paradoxically you will love yourself.

# EMBRACE YOUR FLAWS

*"When you learn to embrace your flaws is how you learn to love yourself, perfectly".*

— *Nyki Edwinna*

Embracing yourself comes when you truly learn to love yourself with all perfections and imperfections. To embrace your imperfections, let go of identifying yourself as inadequate and embody the wholeness of your being.

Consider the accompanying narrative as how our imperfections can be channeled correctly:

A water bearer had two large pots, each hung on the ends of a pole which he carried across his neck. One pot had a crack in it while the other was perfect and consistently delivered a whole portion of water. One day, at the end of the long walk from the stream to his house, the cracked pot arrived half full. This continued daily for two years, with the bearer bringing home one and a half pots of water. The perfect pot was proud of its accomplishments. But the cracked pot was embarrassed by its imperfection since it fulfilled only a fraction of what it was designed for. After two years of enduring this bitter shame, the pot spoke to the water bearer one day by the stream." I am ashamed of myself because the crack in my side causes water to leak the way back to your house". Because of my flaws, you have to do all of this work, and you don't get full value from your efforts. The bearer replied, "Did you notice that there were flowers only on your side of the path, but not on the other pot's side? That's because I've always known about your flaw. I sowed flower seeds on your side of the path and every day on our walk back to the house, you've watered them. For two years I've picked these beautiful flowers to decorate the master's table. Without you being just the way you are, he would not have this beauty to grace his house".

Each of us have flaws. We are all cracked pots. Don't be afraid of your flaws. Learn to accept your body for all the wonderful gifts it brings you and reject the destructive fake images we are bombarded with every day. Acceptance is something we need in life. Until and unless we accept ourselves for the way we are, it is going to be difficult to bring improvement in our life. It doesn't matter whether you are fat or thin, tall or short, strong or weak. It doesn't matter whether you talk less or more, you are not useless. Accept yourself the way you are. Try to shift your focus from being negative to positive. It is not possible to shut out the words of every person who demotivates us, but it is possible to not let them affect you. Nobody, is perfect, not even those who bring us down. Do not define yourself on the basis of others poor judgements about you.

Never compare yourself with another individual with a different set of life experiences, abilities and flaws. If you are comparing yourself with the strength of another person, know that they have their own share of flaws. What we fail to realise is that often the basis of comparison is inappropriate. Don't try to be another person. You might not know, he/she might be struggling with more insecurities and hurdles than you do. This is to remind you once again that a bird cannot be compared to a fish based on their swimming skills.

Negative self-talk to be avoided at all costs. It is any internal dialogue or a voice of the critic, from within oneself, almost like a critical person, constantly reminding yourself of your insecurities, your flaws, your drawbacks and those aspects of you which ultimately limit your potential to reach the zenith. Negative self may sound downright like, "I am not worth anything good in this world" or may sound reasonable like, "I should avoid doing this as it is out of my capacity, just to save myself of humiliation". Every time, the little voice is about to speak up, shut it up by empowering positive self-talk like "I can do it if I try". "I am capable of more than this".

Do you see the same side of the coin when you flip it? If not, the same goes for your flaws. For once, turn your flaws upside down and focus on the positive side of your flaws. If you consider being shy and socially awkward as flaws, remember you could also be a good listener and a keen observer. At the core of this principle is, every individual is unique, with a distinct set of imperfection and near perfections. Letting flaws negatively influence us makes it difficult for us to be happy and sustain our sense of success. Embracing the real you can be difficult and scary at first, it may take a lot of courage. Let go of what others think of you and try to focus on inner self. Embrace your flaws, the change you want in your life and even your fears. It may be difficult and take a long time, but it is not impossible.

That means to love yourself in your entirety. Love every little part of you. Every day, the first thing in the morning even before brushing your teeth, look at yourself in the mirror, intently... Cup your hands around your cheeks, smile and then talk softly to yourself. Say anything — whisper a few loving words — I love you so much... What a treasure you are! Hug yourself... Go crazily creative! Unabashed. Implement this silly game, a few minutes daily. Within a few months, you will find yourself happier and less complaining about your looks. You are as valuable as a whole person, including your imperfections. Trust yourself as you would be a best friend. Other friends may come and go but you're guaranteed to stick around for your entire life. Treat yourself with care and respect and practice positive self-compassion.

## Chapter 06
# FIND YOUR CALLING

# FIND YOUR CALLING

If we are unable to discover our true calling, and waste time and effort in pursuing things which do not motivate us, we will eventually lose faith and confidence in ourselves. Some people find their calling without much effort while others find it after considerable inner churning. But once you find your footing in life, your confidence soars. Bhavan's family expected him to join the family business of manufacturing nuts and bolts. And though he felt obligated to participate in it internally he wasn't happy in doing it. He struggled to find his footing, calling and self-esteem. This turmoil led him to the late Guru Rishi Prabhakar of Siddha Samadhi Yoga ashram in Mumbai. He realised that his heart lay in the study of self and spirituality. Today he is a successful life coach who teaches people the mantra of gaining happiness, success and peace of mind.

## LISTEN TO THE CALL

*"To find your calling,*

*Close your eyes and*

*Look into your heart."*

*— Ken Streator*

What is calling you? Whenever I ask people this question, the first response I often get is nervous laughter, and then a look that says, you don't expect me to answer that, do you? It is not people who don't want to answer, they are just too taken back with the nature of question. It is true, it is a hard question to answer. In order to answer, what is calling you, it deserves some consideration and contemplation. Imagine that this question may be just the beginning probe that will encourage you to start to make an enquiry into your own heart to find an answer. There was a time in my life, not so long ago, that I didn't know what was calling me nor did I know how to figure it out I did not have any experiences that I was aware of, to help me define it for myself. So how, do we know what might be calling us? There is volume of books written on this very subject to give insight and guidance into how one might begin to find their calling. While I am not an expert on the subject, I do not know that there is no right or wrong way to go about the process because it is as unique and individual as each person. There are many hints of calls, it may be internal knowing that points the way to your life's vocation or something much smaller that help you guide you to the next phase or experience.

## HOW TO FIND THE CALLING

I think one of the most important thing you can do is to find time to be quiet every day. This is the time set aside where you will not be interrupted and you can have an open and honest dialogue with yourself. Every day we hear the voice of spirit if we stop to listen. It comes as soft whispers of opportunity and choices or perhaps it is an internal knowing that we cannot deny. Everything that comes our way, every experience, gives us an opportunity to make a choice of how we respond to create our life. That is where the calling... in the experience of everyday life. When we choose to pay attention to our life, ask for guidance and listen to our heart, it will lead us to the right direction.

## PRESERVE YOUR ORIGINALITY

*"Drop the idea of becoming someone,*
*because you are already a masterpiece.*
*You cannot be improved.*
*You have only to come to it,*
*to know it, to realise it."*

— *Osho*

Everything has an essential property and a non-essential property. For instance, chillness is the essential property of ice. Ice can have many non-essential properties; it can have the shape of ice cubes, ice bars, powdered ice, snow etc. But there cannot be hot ice. The entire struggle of life comes when somehow one attempts to make ice hot. That is walking into failure because that is against its essential property. In the case of a person if he tries to go against the essential nature, struggle is inevitable. Eventually on looking back even a sense of failure may set it. You are not designed or destined to fail, it is not you lack capabilities or potential; but just that you attempted to live an entire life against your very nature. The essential nature of each one of you has to be discovered and you need to live by it; choose actions or professions that go with this fundamental basic nature in you. Some of you are natural businessman and that is what should be; some of you are dancers you have to do whatever in life through dance; some of you are born teachers, some of you are born to be sales person, so on and so forth. You have to observe what your essential nature is and discover it over a period of time. Initially you will know what is not your essential property; eliminate what you are not till you can find out what you are and then live a life aligned to that real nature in you. On all the non-essential aspects of life adapt to the world; on all essential nature of yours, teach the world to adapt to you. Becoming the Being you were designed to be, i.e. ever connected to your divine route, is spirituality. Do not move away from your being, move into your being. Preserve that originality and see how life unfolds for you.

In short, if you ever find yourself in minority, you are in the right place. Don't complain about it. Yes, you will find yourself alone sometimes, but it's okay. The world will first laugh at you and for the very reason that world will start looking up to you, it will accept and admire you later. *"Each work has to pass through these stages—ridicule, opposition and then acceptance. Those who think ahead of their times are sure to be misunderstood."* says Swami Vivekananda.

# Chapter 07
## GIFTS TO GIVE YOURSELF

# GIFTS TO GIVE YOURSELF

*"The most valuable gift you have to offer is yourself"*

— *Bob Burg*

Is my life style so very turbo changed? Am I wearing my busyness as badges of honour? Am I slowly drifting away from the path of a powerful and meaningful life? Am I deprived of the quality ME time? Myriad thoughts ranted in my head. Every moment is perfectly new in its own way, carrying its own charm. Incredible things begin to happen when you start investing in time for yourself and living it fully. In this way, we don't end up missing half the future in the hurry to get there. The best gifts you can give yourself are things that are priceless. They are collection of moments and experiences that add depths and value to your life.

## 'ME —TIME' IS IMPORTANT

*""Me" time is just as important as "us" time"*

— *Chris Pine*

'Me — Time' is the simple act of becoming conscious of something - you may notice that you don't feel right physically and emotionally, maybe you catch a judgemental thought or feel the beginning of a knot in your stomach. Now that you are aware of it, you can learn from it and do something to shift the effect. Awareness is the first step in any change process. "What I am thinking and feeling?" may be a useful question that you could ask yourself. 'Me time' is important and make sure to take a break every moment then to just do what makes you happy. If you are replacing something you love with something that you are not fond of, it won't work in long time. Keep something that you love doing in your routine. This will help you set your own standards and boundaries which are hopefully signed with your values, so that you can create the life you want. Perhaps! It's time to learn and reconnect yourself, more productive, more energy.

## LIVE YOUR DREAM

*"The best gift that you can give yourself is the gift of possibility"*

— *Paul Newman*

Possibilities fructify only if we hold on to our dreams, even if our path may have several bends. Gift yourself the gift following your dreams. There was a time when my life had only three things — that greatest power above, God, me and that belief in my writing. When I started to fall in love with life all over again; I started living on my own terms. I felt that all those who told me that what I was doing was a waste of time, or who asked me what I would achieve through writing, probably got the best answer ever. And now I am giving myself a chance to do what it is I love. I also realised the power of inner desire, the power of visualising a dream. All I can now say is just dream big and follow your heart. I converted my dreams to action which is to help others whose lights have been dimmed to find purpose and passion again.

## PEACE OF MIND

*'Peace of Mind, the greatest gift you can give yourself'*

— *Connor Tim*

Everything is meaningful only in the context of peace. Let peace be the constant and let everything else be a variable. To be peaceful you have to take care of your physical well-being. So, invest one hour a day on the body and cherish the benefit of it during the remaining twenty-three hours. Predominantly be attracted by health-conscious foods and only occasionally be distracted by tongue conscious food. To be peaceful, you must enjoy work. Find a work that gives you inner expression. You find fulfilment in it. Make the world recognise the value you add by your work. You will find success in it. You will find peace through your work. Make this work of yourself useful to the world. You will find your life's purpose in it. To be peaceful, you must invest in silence. The cluttered mind needs quiet moments. Franz Kafka so eloquently put it: "It is not necessary that you leave the house. Remain at your table and listen. Do not even wait; be wholly, still and alone. The world will present itself to you for its unmasking, it can do no other, in ecstasy it will writhe at your feet". Let all your doing be punctuated by non-doing. Even if you have not been initiated into meditation, at least practice stillness, every day. Focus on present moment and count the blessings. Have faith. Connect that's beyond your judgement. Play the game of your life to your heart's content... play right... play it peacefully. Play it for peace. Play it with peace.

## FORGIVENESS

> *"It's one of the greatest gift you can give yourself. To forgive. Forgive everybody."*
>
> *— Maya Angelou*

Forgiveness is basically a healing tool both for oneself and for the other. The raging thoughts that emerge from within are not our doing as they have their own energy and momentum. Our responsibility is not to be overpowered by them and allow them to destroy our peace of mind. For instance, we often have a hard time forgiving ourselves for our mistakes. Stop berating yourself and your actions. Forgive and let go of the guilt and shame, yet give yourself the power to change your story. Be nice to yourself. When you catch yourself taking negatively, change it to a more positive and supportive voice. The tool we should use to do this is forgiveness. Forgiveness to others is a means of letting go feelings vindictiveness, rebuilding trust, regaining the sense of belonging, freeing the other of guilt and freeing oneself from anger and resentment.

## TIME TO LEARN ABOUT YOURSELF

*"Often the best gift you can give yourself is time alone — some time to ask your questions and listen quietly for answers"*

*— Katrina Meyer*

Give yourself the permission to explore and really get to know who you are. Discover what you like and don't like. This will help you set your own standards and boundaries which are hopefully signed with your values, so that you can create the life you want. According to Rhonda Britten's quotes — *"If you value yourself, you understand that you are a gift to anyone you meet".* Along the way you might find that things change. And that's okay. It's natural. When it does, recognise this and be mindful in your daily actions as you adjust to the person you are becoming. Gift yourself 'off' screen times. Set yourself a time for using digital devices.

## SELF-REFLECTION

*"Time spent in self-reflection is never wasted— it is an intimate date with yourself".*

*— Paul TP Wong*

We are mostly so caught up in daily hassles of the mundane world, that we forget the 'fundamentals'. We forget to pause and appreciate nature, we forget to thank our loved ones and tell them how much they mean to us. We forget to focus on what really matters to us. Self-reflection brings close to ourselves and help to gain clarity over emotions. Coupled with positivity and candid mindfulness. It gets us close to recognising the good and bad inside. It leads us to an awareness of our self and it is more connecting with the inner-self. It is basically giving careful thought to your own behaviour and beliefs. At the end of the day, it's all in your mind. Let's all choose to take stress-free time for ourselves often, so we don't fall in a 'rut'.

In short don't wait for gifts from your loved ones just on your special occasions but cherish every gift that has been bestowed upon us by the Creator. Start every new day, gifted to you as an empty canvas, by embracing the positive outlook and excitement to live every moment with vibrant colours, jubilant spirit, smiling heart, fill the canvas with new work that has never been done. Like every drop of water forms ocean, compiling every day lived enthusiastically, outweighing triumph leads to wonderful cherishing days. You are rich by what you are. The best gift that you can give is a little bit of your own care and attention.

# Chapter 08
# HEAL YOURSELF

## HEAL YOURSELF

*"My whole life I kept making the mistake of cleaning the mirror without realising that my own face was tarnished"*

— *Mirza Ghalib*

Did you know that harnessing the power of our mind, we heal ourselves? How does this work? When the individual believes that the medicine will create some effect, the body's chemical mechanism must react to produce some results. The body will release some feel-good hormones which can give a positive feeling about the whole thing. So, stop feeling like a victim of life and take charge of your mind, body and thoughts. The solutions are simpler than the problems we are facing. Self-healing is a soul-bathing process. Every cell of our body is communicating a story, and we start the journey by listening to our thoughts. What produces these effects? Our expectations and beliefs. The belief that the medicine will work is creating the result of what is expected. How does belief work?

*"The mind of the man is the man; the power of the mind is in power of the subconscious mind".*

— *Mahatria*

*Yes! All of us have specific beliefs when it comes to the body and illness...*

*"If I take pain killers, the side effects will be more..."*

*"My work is everything to me. If I go to work, I will be okay..."*

*"If I follow holistic therapies like yoga and meditation, everything will be ok..."*

*If I repeat positive affirmations, I will become alright..."*

Like this, the list of beliefs can be endless and very subjective. These beliefs become very strong over a period of time since they are repeated 'N' number of times. And our subconscious mind has the power to manifest our beliefs. The power of subconscious mind has the potential to heal ourselves. So, in the above examples, it is not the painkillers effect or exercises or affirmations that works. It is the belief that is producing the expected results. There is a deep connection between a person's emotional and mental state and the diseases they carry. Whenever a person comes down with any disease, they need to look at what they have been thinking or what emotions they have been suppressing. It's about replacing our negative thoughts with positive thoughts and affirmations can bring back good health. But so often we get lost in the vicious cycle of negative thoughts. From a student to a professional to a homemaker, all of us go through negative thoughts. Surprising our beliefs, emotions, thoughts together equals to reality of miraculous healing.

## YOUR BODY CAN HEAL YOURSELF

*"The more consciousness you bring into your body, the stronger your immune system becomes. It is as if every cell awakens and rejoices. Your body loves your attention. It is also a potent form of self-healing".*

— *Eckhart Tolle*

Our body has a defense mechanism which probably has been taken for granted; the day to day functioning seldom makes us sit down and observe some of these defense mechanisms which keep us healthy. Nature has inbuilt ways to heal us and yet sadly what most people do is numb their bodies with painkillers. We have forgotten to listen to our own body and override all sorts of artificial chemicals and natural therapies. Let's see some of the basic healing that our body does for us...

## BODY HEALS WHILE STRETCHING

First thing that we do unconsciously after we wake up is to stretch ourselves. It increases blood flow to the muscles and helps them get back work when we feel lethargic. This movement heals the body and flex.

## BODY HEALS IN TEARS

We have seen tears of joy, hurt, loss. The mucous membrane of our eyes is very delicate and needs protection from foreign objects. Tears protect our eyes from any foreign object that touches our eye balls.

## BODY HEALS WHEN YOU BREATHE FRESH AIR

We can live for a few minutes without air. After you take in air through lungs, your red blood cells pick up the oxygen and carry it to the rest of cells in your body. Your cells then use this steady supply of oxygen in an energy producing process called metabolism. Every time you breathe out through your lungs, you let out toxins. These wastes are by products of the metabolism that is constantly taking place in your cells. If you are always breathing in stale air, you are depriving your cells of one of the most basic need. If your cells get enough oxygen, they will be healthy. Healthy cells make up a healthy body. Breathing fresh air can heal you.

## BODY HEALS WHILE SLEEPING

Our body is endlessly working to repair and regenerate itself. This happens to a great extent while we are sleeping. If you don't get adequate sleep, you could find yourself sick a lot.

## BODY HEALS WHEN YOU SNEEZE

Our body is incredible in its design; there are many organisms which keep on trying to attack our body. Our body is saving us from bacterial attack. Whenever our nasal passage gets filled with too many allergens, dust or other foreign particles, sneezing helps us to get rid of them. Something as simple as sneezing can heal our body.

## LISTEN TO YOUR BODY WHILE HICCUPS

Most often hiccups occur when we tend to eat fast or over eat and it annoys your health. So, if you get hiccups while eating, body is saying slow down your eating. These are defense mechanisms of the body and we need to listen to them and move accordingly.

## BODY HEALS WHEN WE ARE AROUND OPTIMISTIC PEOPLE

To be healthy is not just about food and exercise; it's about whom you relate with on a daily basis. When you relate with people who all the time talk about issues, sickness, and problems, it can deplete your energy levels. As a counter measure, surround yourself with optimistic and humorous people.

## WHAT IS FAITH HEALING?

*"Healing necessitates a fearless connection to the Divine, strong faith, and commitment to living your truth in the world"*

— *Wendy De Rosa*

We would have experienced the feel-good effect while saying our prayers or while visiting places of worship or being in presence of evolved souls. In those moments there is a gush of energy pouring on us since there energy levels are very high. This gush of energy has potential to put our conscious mind off (the thinking mind). So, we will be in a state either null of thoughts or less of thoughts. In those moments we will get in touch with our subconscious mind. In that stage subconscious mind will be in a state of absolute readiness to enhance the natural healing process. What we receive tend to loss after sometime. So, just as we need the reservoir to save natural resources, we also need a reservoir to save energy, the enhancer of natural healing. Meditation can act like the reservoir. Through meditation we can connect to the gushing energy which can fill us with healing energy.

## SELF-HEALING

In the midst of the crowd, you are still existentially alone. You are the architect, creator and harbinger of your life. Once you are enabled to make your decisions with simplicity and speed, you will see the power and effectiveness of self-healing. Well, Louise Hay's teachings are her loving gifts of inspiration which shall continue to guide our lives and teach us to become more loving and accepting of ourselves and others. Healing her own cancer, Louise L Hay, the goddess of self-love, passed away peacefully in her sleep on August 30, 2017 at her residence in San Diego, USA. She was 90. Struck by cancer, Louise overcame the terrible disease by using only alternative methods such as positive affirmations, nutritional cleansing, visualisation and psychotherapy to heal herself. This sent out a clear message to everyone that we are all personally responsible for our health and healing. It also proved what Louise was emphasising in her philosophy— that the body knows how to heal itself, provided we listen to it and support it in loving ways. Her recovery from cancer paved the way for her greatest offering in the form of her book, You Can Heal Your Life, that went on to transform the lives of uncountable people on the planet.

## NATURE THE ETERNAL HEALER

*"I firmly believe that nature brings solace in all troubles"*

— *Anne Frank*

Many diseases can be prevented if we take even short one-day breaks in the lap of Mother Nature. It is neutral; hence it absorbs a lot of our negative vibrations. It helps us to empty ourselves and fills us with positivity, peace — through the application of nature's wonders in the form of Ayurveda, Unani, and naturopathy. However, when we root ourselves in nature, we do not specifically require healing through nature because we are already healing with nature. "When one can be in awe of the mystery and beauty of life there tends to be healing and a well-being which includes hope, calmness, and trust in life. This is something which is not objectively measurable; it can only be experienced. This healing benefits people's psycho-emotional, physical, social and spiritual well-being". Moreover, regular exposure to nature has well-known mental and physical health benefits especially in kids. It is linked to reduced ADHD, more creativity, better critical thinking, better behaviour test scores, and even a stronger sense of purpose. Nature has its own way of communicating. Just pay attention and an attitude of gratitude to Mother Nature "Thank you for being so unconditionally loving, giving and nourishing our soul." We live once and to live healthy is our prime responsibility. Just remember that you do one of the two things every day: you either build health or disease in yourself. Let's believe in the healing abilities of the body before popping medicines.

# Chapter 09
# I AM POSSIBLE

# I AM POSSIBLE

*"Nothing is impossible
the word itself says
'I'm possible"*

— *Audrey Hepburn*

Everyone is working towards reinventing themselves without being limited by age or their given situation. Things have changed. There is nothing impossible about change anymore. The unbearable weight the word 'change' once carried along with it has been lifted. Change to people in our times is not what it used to be for our parents: a frightening thought and a challenging path that could be taken only if it was the last choice. Today everyone wants to change the fundamental aspect of themselves. To be specific, they want to move towards the positive, and be more open, extroverted, and more agreeable.

## HOW TO REINVENT YOURSELF

*"If you want a new outcome,
You will have to break the
Habit of being yourself
And reinvent a new self."*

— *Dr. Joe Dispenza*

The rules for reinvention have changed. Whether you want to end procrastinating or become more sociable, it's possible to change the very basic idea of who you are. It means letting go of stuff that is currently holding you back. Otherwise letting go of outdated habits, routines, roles and responsibilities that keep you from living life to fullest. It means making a new set of choices and forging down a new path that expands opportunities, options and possibilities. You want to reinvent yourself; you need will and action. Doing something bold. To have a desire to live your life, not just exist between the grind of earning your bread and butter. And to change yourself, requires you to go through a process of self-discovery. It means setting a new set of goals and objectives, and then drawing out a plan for achieving them. This, of course, will require building a set of patterns and behaviours that are aligned with the goals you want to achieve.

## CRUSH REGRET AND RESTART ANYTIME

Anything is possible anytime. If you decide to transform yourself, you can do it anytime. Anytime is awesome! I believe anyone at any time can make a change to their lives if they want to enough. The key phrase here is "if you want to enough". Surprise others. Because they might have developed fixed ideas about who you are and what you are capable of doing. If you want to reinvent yourself, you need to upend those assumptions and hopefully do it in a dramatic way, so they are sure to notice. Entrepreneur Bhavik Vasa's mother became a Sanskrit teacher at age 54 and his father has discovered running and half-marathons as his hobby at age 62. Change comes with micro steps.

## BOOST YOUR MASTERY—AT ANYTHING

Self-mastery is master yourself to the challenges, the hardcore of time of making a difficult and quick decision. You can absolutely be mastering the circumstances and be experiencing the changes that you wanted to see. It is having control over what we really want, the outcome we are looking for to the end of the result. We understand who we are and what we are capable of without any doubt, because we fully regain control over it. The desire for change comes from within to attain any dream and goals.

## LOSS THE FEAR OF DISAPPOINTMENT

When you overly personalise a disappointment, you make it about who you are as a person and do not take into account the many situational factors that had nothing to do with you. If you apply for a job but don't receive an interview, there were likely many qualified applicants for the position, or maybe they had already hired someone before the job was even listed. The point here is there are always situational factors that influence any event. Additionally, whether or not a situation works out the way you want it nothing about your worthiness then or in future.

## BUILD FAITH IN YOURSELF

There are no untested legends. The strength of character is derived from the strength of faith... not necessarily in God but 'faith in something'. You got to believe in something beyond yourself. Win in your mind first. Stay enthusiastic. Invert your thinking. Develop competence. Focus on positive. Go for it.

## DON'T BE JUDGMENTAL

It is one of the primary criteria to changing. You must be less judgmental, care fewer what others think of you. To be non-judgmental, there has to be total acceptance and zero expectations. Such a person does not come from any projections as to how life or people should be or should not be. Such a mind is expansive and is able to accommodate a large variety of situations, personality types and behaviour traits.

## SUPPORT

Although it is important that you learn to rely on yourself when facing any challenge, it is also important to have a support team that you can lean on to give a boost when things get too tough and correct you when you're making mistakes. Don't maintain social connections with your own age group: meet and get to know people across generations.

## HAVE COURAGE AND A PLAN

Internally you have an intense desire to change, but externally, things are just not panning out as you had expected. Then you need to potentially give up things that you have been clinging onto many years. Likewise, you might need to muster up courage to do things that normally just don't feel comfortable pursuing. This will also require a great deal of mental energy, planning and focus.

## LEAVE YOUR COMFORT ZONE

Keep challenging. Challenge society's stereotyping of who you are. That means you will need to actively stretch your comfort zone and proactively push yourself in a brand-new direction. It can be as difficult as kicking a vice, but a new self-image will always remind you of why you're trying to change.

## AGE NO BAR

*"You are never too old to reinvent yourself"*

— *Steve Harvey*

Ageing is a process of opening rather than closing doors. Age is no bar to chase your dreams on yourself. It just takes willpower and discipline to achieve the impossible. At 102, Indian Man Kaur runs marathon races. She started running when she was 93. She wanted to change her sedentary life and made sure she practiced every day. And she took up the challenge, at the urging of her son and hasn't looked back since, adding javelin and shot put to her repertoire. Now she has clinched her second successive medal at the World Marathon Athletics Championship in Malaga Spain. Her mantra may not be too set in your ways. Always be open and flexible to experimenting with good things.

You can rise up from anything. You can completely recreate yourself. Nothing is permanent. You are not stuck. You have choices. You can think new thoughts. You can learn something new. You can create new habits. All that matters is that you decide today and never look back. Every day is a chance to reinvent yourself and become brand new. Every next level of your life will demand a different version of you. Nothing is impossible if you believe. There are things inside, you never knew you had. Step out. Your future depends on the choices you make right now...

## Chapter 10
# JUST LAUGH IT AWAY

## JUST LAUGH IT AWAY

*""Men's best successes come after their*

*"Disappointments"*

*Disappointment is the nurse of wisdom""*

— Bayle Roche

It would be a rare day in our lives if we could live 24 hrs without having to deal with some or the other types of disappointments. The chances that our expectations will not be met each day by individuals, governments, clients, vendors, organisations, family members and the like are very likely. In fact, as you mature through the life cycle, it seems you are likely to be let down in some way by at least a simple majority of people you come in contact with. Did you ever stop to think why you are disappointed so often? Is it happening to you or everyone around you? Are you doing something wrong? May be! Have you taken the time to understand that you will be disappointed often and that you will be prepared to deal with disappointment?

### THE BURDEN OF EXPECTATION

*"If you expect nothing, you can never be disappointed."*

— *Tonya Huxley*

Can you expect everyone to make you happy? Do you do the same? Are you wondering if your expectations are too high? For instance, my friend expected her boss to appreciate her hard work for giving the output before time. Well, he didn't say a word over it and... whoosh! There came the disappointment. I expected my husband to do something, but he didn't! Well, I quickly boiled up! I didn't expect someone to be harsh on me with their words, and they did. Ah! There came the tears as swiftly as my pizza order. Well, even takes 30 minutes but tears, not even 30 seconds! I realised the causes, the triggers. All I had to do was find a solution. At first, the solution seemed "Don't expect". But alas, our expectations rise like dawn and fall like dusk to bring in disappointment. You will end up really disappointed if you think people will do for you as you do for them. Not everyone has the same heart as you. Don't blame people for disappointing you, blame yourself for expecting too much from them. Never get too attached to anyone, it will lead to expectations and expectations always lead to disappointment. Anticipate everything and expect nothing. The same goes for unpleasant situations, things and people. It can never remain under your control, only 'YOU' can. The message that this phrase furnishes is no less than a precious pearl in an oyster. A strong urge to have everything under control, or wanting things to happen as per our expectations, sow the seed of reaction. When expectation falls to meet reality, we become insane about being out of control, and thus we react.

## HERE IS A SIMPLE 3-STEP PROCESS TO TRANSFORM FROM BEING A REACTOR TO CREATOR:

1. Observation: Whatever the situation is, observe it neutrally. Neutrally means observing 'What is' instead of thinking 'What can be' or 'What should be'. We always tend to create a hotchpotch of reality with our expectations.
2. Perception: A pinch of salt in a glass will make the water salty, but a pinch of salt will not affect the taste of water in an enormous river. With an enhanced perception, you can access multiple approaches.

3. Creation: As you observe the reality and broaden your perception, you will be able to create something out of any situation. No matter what situations you are faced with, you will be able to take the path of 'Creation' instead of ' Reaction'.

## SELF-ACCEPTANCE

*"When you learn to accept instead of expect... you'll have fewer disappointments".*

*— Robert Fisher*

Through acceptance one rise above being a victim of circumstances and become a victor instead. Acceptance is a powerful weapon that grant the true success in life. When we accept the relationship as it is and also the other person's reactivity completely, we offer the space to experience their feelings fully and to heal from them. Once this has been done, and it will take time, the relationship will not only resume but also do so at a for higher level than before. If we stop fretting about a certain situation and accept it fully instead, we open ourselves to remarkable creative possibilities. When life offers us a lemon, we lose no time in making lemonade, lemon pickle, lemon chutney, or in growing a lemon orchard. Thus, I realised the only thing that stays in my hand is acceptance. If I accept people the way they are, then my disappointment level would swoop to nothing. The more I accept the lesser the disappointment. The more I accept, the happier I am! The more I focus on giving, the less I worry about getting.

## CHOOSE TO BE HAPPY

*"If we magnified our successes as much as we magnify our disappointments, we'd all be much happier"*

— *Abraham Lincoln*

It is within your power to have the determination of an ant, who find a way to accomplish its mission, regardless of the obstacles it faces. Your reaction to disappointment is where your power lies. And whether you want to admit to it or not, it is you who choose how you are going to react. No one can make you react a certain way. Everything depends on what you want. Many times, reactions are learned. If your father slammed the phone down when he is angry, you may have learned to do the same thing. Well to begin with, if you want to live a happier life, it is best to choose a peaceful reaction to life's disappointments. If you are constantly yelling and upset about how someone else messed up, then your proclamations of wanting to be a happy person are just hot air! If you want to be happy — prove it. Joy, love, contentment bolsters your physical being, while negative emotions like anger and stress cause all types of harm and imbalance to our self. So, imagine this: You live in a world where mistakes are made and will always be made. Would it be logical if every time someone makes a mistake, or causes disappointments, for you to choose (through your emotions) to mentally and physically harm yourself? What will you achieve by that? You should not harm anyone, let alone yourself. Try to be more prepared for the disappointments. Disappointments will always come your way. Choose to be happy! Have the mindset to laugh it off and persist to overcome any disappointment. Gently lean into your pain rather than run from it. You are much stronger than you think. I view that freedom of choice to be extremely powerful and liberating. It lends truth to the saying, "Happiness is a choice". It hurts to let go, but sometimes it hurts more to hold on. Disappointments will always come your way, just laugh it away!

# Chapter 11
# KNOW(ING)! THE SELF

# KNOW(ING)! THE SELF

*"Knowing Yourself is the beginning of all wisdom"*

— *Aristotle*

## KNOWING IS A PRESENT CONTINUOUS.....PROCESS.

I love enjoying a good South Indian filter coffee. Although I drink utmost 5 to 6 cups a week and yet I am very particular about the temperature and aroma of a good coffee. I look forward to having a good coffee in my office cafeteria which has a South Indian filter coffee counter serving one of the best coffees to my taste. It's an experience I cherish the most. Once I thought to prepare coffee at home as well. Immediately I went on a coffee-making shopping spree to get the relevant material viz. coffee filter, coffee powder and so on. But it was never 100% of my preference and over a period of time, I did trial and error method only to settle for something close to 95% of what tasted the best for me. Then when I enquired about the reasons for this variation, I came to know from the coffee vendor that there are many factors in preparing a coffee, in terms of quality of milk, combination of coffee brew, moisture of coffee powder, proportion of milk, sugar and so on. This provided the insight for me that it is just that they know how to make a good coffee; it is their ability of knowing the process it takes to get to the perfection and that is a continuous process.

Even a Michael Phelps who is considered one of the fastest living swimmers in the world will not say 'I know swimming' even for him it is a process of continuous improvement which means he is also 'knowing...' in the present continuous. I can never say I know; we can only say 'knowing' because the process is evolution towards that infinite state. 'I know' state of mind is a self-fulfilling prophecy, where as 'knowing' is a journey towards infinite possibilities which reveals itself to the one who seeks. This is the state of staying humble with a conviction to give the best. Thus to make this job easy for you, below are some classic ways to evaluate yourself without any bias which will help to reach your professional and personal goals. Ask yourself thoughtful questions:

1. What do you love to do?
2. What are your dreams in life?
3. What do you want your legacy to be?
4. What is your biggest criticism of yourself?
5. What are some mistakes you've made?
6. How do others perceive you? How would you like them to perceive you?
7. Who is your role model?

## STEPS TO "KNOWING THE SELF":

### Never Fear

*"If you look into your own heart, and you find nothing wrong there, what is there to worry about? What is there to fear?"*

*— Confucius*

Don't be afraid of your fears, they're there to let you know that something is worth of it. To know yourself, look at your fears. Being fearless is a state of mind, though it needs to be developed and practiced. However, fearlessness emerging out of arrogance is not a virtue. It is pure, when it mellows out of love and diligence. Being fearless is synonymous with bravery, heroism, and fortitude. Fear hinders our growth, it's like a wall between our abilities and our dreams and keep us away from happiness. Being righteous means being fearless by following our inner voice, thus being established in our true state. We just have to be fearful of one thing— hurting others. It is belief which makes us fearless; so, believe in morality, dharma, and love to make yourself fearless.

## Never Compare

*"Don't compare yourself with anyone in this world... if you do so, you are insulting yourself".*

— *Bill Gates*

We are one and only legitimate frame of reference. So, it will help if we track ourselves against our own self of yesterday. Here a little self-love can go a long way when it comes to liberating ourselves from the shackles that comparison wraps around our psyche. When comparing ourselves to others, we sometimes feel like we've missed the boat'. It's a thought that break resignation and fuels self-pity. In reality there is no boat! We are the only boat in our life. There is no other boat! We do need a benchmark as a tool to progress in life but this happens only when we focus on our own progress. We must commit to working hard to take of ourselves physically, emotionally and spiritually. This results in us growing in all areas a little bit each day. Along with this, we could celebrate the little advancements we are making without comparing with others. Let us remember that we all have our own mountains to climb, fears to conquer and paths to forge. Knowing this, let us run our own race and let others run theirs. Thus, comparison is a joy thief and a happiness killer.

## Be Honest

*"Honesty and transparency make you vulnerable. Be honest and transparent anyway".*

— *Mother Theresa*

The most important thing is to always be honest with yourself about the things that matter, without that, you have nothing. And the most honest convictions you'll have is with yourself, because you'll always know when you are lying. Be true to the situation and not to your personal likes and dislikes. The personality lives off emotional swings— between what you like and what you don't like. It uses the dynamic pendulum to keep itself going. You can't be sure of your likes and dislikes. So be true to the situation, to the event or circumstances you're facing. What does the situation require? It might not be what suits you personally. For example, if you're employed to do a job, be true to what you're paid for, not to whether you like it or don't like it. If you insist on reacting in dislike, be true to the situation and resign, because clearly you won't be doing a good job.

Give up being dishonest to yourself and your life. Any time you're angry, resentful or depressed, it means you are not being honest: you are not facing life it is. Anger arises because you are not getting your own way. Instead of being angry, you should be looking at what practical action you can take to get around the obstruction. If there's no practical action you can take, your desire is impractical at this time. To be honest you must face the fact and give up your wanting. If you want to be trusted, be honest. If you want to be honest, be true. If you want to be true, be yourself.

## See yourself as others see you

*"The more you know yourself, the more patience you have for what you see in others".*

— Erik Erikson

"To see ourselves as others see us is a most salutary gift. Hardly less important is the capacity to see others as they see themselves". I accepted that I suffered from aggression, guilt, envy and insecurity. Once I accepted these negative emotions about myself, because acceptance is important and stopped giving myself a hard time for it, things changed. I let go off trying to control others around me to be the way I wanted to be, my way, the right way. Instead, I started accepting them for who they were. That was peace started trickling in, I stopped wasting precious energy on voicing my opinions vehemently and I started focusing on myself, my issues, and my insecurities. Only once I got to the bottom of it, did I start slowly but surely, loving myself. Through acceptance one acquires the key to creative possibilities and higher levels of being. One rise above being a victim of circumstances and become a victor instead. In this zone, life takes on a magical quality, for life and you are creators and change happens smoothly, harmoniously and swiftly.

## Get feedback about yourself from others

*"Knowing how you want your work to look helps you decide who best to work with and where".*

— Michele Jennae

Sherlock Holmes was a brilliant detective. But even he needed to bounce ideas off Dr. Watson at times. Some people prefer to work alone. I am one of them and maybe you are too. But if you don't work as part of a team, getting someone else's opinion of your work can help you focus your thinking and produce ideas you hadn't thought of. Take the feedback for what it's worth. If you feel you are right, and the criticisms are off base, ignore them. But more often than not, feedback will provide useful information that can help you come with the best most profitable idea. One good guide: if only one reviewer complains about a particular item, you can ignore it. But if all three reviewers make the same comment, they're probably on to something and you should take a closer look.

## Incorporate mindfulness into your day

*"Mindfulness means paying attention in a particular way; on purpose, in the present moment; and non-judgmentally".*

— *Jon Kabat-Zinn*

Most of us tend to be wallow-ers or wait-ers. The wallow-ers carry into each moment baggage from the past. Guilt, resentments, grievance, sadness, bitterness, and forgiveness typify the wallow-er mindset. The wait-er mindset is typical of those who are busy getting to the future — that perfect job, house or relationship — that the present is reduced to a mere means of reaching there. Unease, anxiety, tension, stress, and worry go with living too much in the future. Recognising which side one tends towards, is an important first step towards mindfulness. Thus, cultivating present moment awareness is a technique that could help you realise your own highest potential. And practice of specific techniques incorporated into daily living like meditation into daily living can also provide a way forward. It is essential to bring consciousness into your life in ordinary situations when everything is going relatively smoothly. In this way you grow in the present moment.

## Identity your Body Image

*"You are imperfect, permanently and inevitably flawed and you are beautiful"*

— *Amy Bloom*

Body image is mental and emotional: it's both the mental picture that you have of your body and the way you feel about your body when you look in a mirror. Healthy body image is more than simply tolerating yourself what you look like or not disliking "yourself". A healthy body image means you truly accept and like the way you look right now, and aren't trying to change your body to fit the way you think you should look. It means recognising the individual qualities and strengths that make you feel good about yourself beyond weight, shape or appearance and resisting the pressure to strive for the myth of the 'perfect' body that you see in the media, online, in your communities. If you don't like your body, it is hard to feel good about your whole self.

## Write a journal everyday

*"Though no one can go back and make a brand-new start, anyone can start from now and make a brand-new ending"*

— *Carl Bard*

Writers have written journals for as long as they have written books. Mental health professionals recommend journal writing to patients dealing with anxiety, depression and high stress. Many successful people vouch for this technique to keep their heads clear and focus on their work. Growing up most of us have written a 'diary' in which we have poured all our deepest and darkest secrets. Writing journal will help you clear your thoughts. A lot of us get busy with everyday life our thoughts get muggy. We get so caught up in the daily grind that we lose touch with who we are. Secondly it will help you process things much better. The more you learn about who you are and how you think, the more authentic a life you can live. Journaling helps us process what happens in our lives, and figure out how we feel about those things. Thirdly, it relieves from stress. Writing everything down is also a process of relieving cathartic experience. Moreover, journaling will be a record of your life. It is a humbling experience to know and remember the journey. Imagine opening your journal in the later stage of life, reliving all the moments of victory and defeat that no longer matter.

*"Knowing yourself and asking self-evaluation questions is an important part of the process"*

— Misti Patrella

## Chapter 12

# LIVING WITH THE REAL YOU
# LIVE BEFORE YOU LEAVE
# LIFT YOURSELF BY YOURSELF

# LIVING WITH THE REAL YOU

*"To thine own self be true"*

— *Shakespeare*

When I started my writing journey, I sought acceptance - of my work and thoughts. My mind ticked and my heart skipped a beat, waiting anxiously to glean the feedback. I used to let the feedback affect me and I would wonder, "Why am I not like others?" Later on, things changed. Now I am a person completely open to feedback. Anyone can give me a feedback and I take it willingly. To date, I have never failed to take feedback and process it. Thus, I remained open to feedback from anyone but the way I processed it changed completely. Rather than condemning myself, I take in the feedback, analyse it and see it if it will make me a better person. If so, then the implementation of feedback starts. As I gained maturity through life experiences, the way I process feedback also has gone through enhancement. Any feedback that attempts to change the core of who I am gets rejected immediately. Over time, I just know that this feedback is to be rejected straight away and I just do that. I don't work upon them or get worked up! After years and years of trying to fit in where I don't belong, after years of living as a copy rather than an original version of me, after years of being judged and, criticised, after years of feeling rejected and being so hard on myself, for the first time after so many years, I feel liberated in saying, " I will not change for anyone or anything." Does that mean I am perfect? Never! The mortal me, is never free from defects. I am not making an excuse for limitations. Every limitation of mine has to be overcome and the striving continues in the aspects of my limitations and weakness. But I will not change who I am for anyone or for anything.

Secondly, ask yourself whether you are happy with others than yourself… I believe the question would be a bit rhetorical, leading to a yes. Truly speaking we all experience a sense of void or, rather, incompleteness within ourselves, thus getting accustomed to the belief that we need one more chunk to finish our cake. Often, we feel someone is better than us, but will we hold onto ourselves there? No. When someone does something better than us, we scale them up by pushing ourselves down. Thus, we end up either turning much too humble or contemplate aping things which they deem worth of considering. Our entire life, we are worried about what the world thinks about us… discusses and says about us. When we look into ourselves, we meet all our expectations we have for ourselves. We want to exercise, but do not do it. We want to have healthy food; we do not do it. We want to be on time but procrastinate all times. We do not meet our own expectations, but still we expect the world outside to meet our expectations. What an irony! In this way, we are not able to see ourselves for what we are; what we are looking for is ourselves in the eyes of others. This is what makes it arduous for most of us to respond to the question: "Tell about yourself", because, even we are not certain about the way we live our life. Our value always depends on how much we value ourself. If you believe that what is innately yours needs someone's evaluation to be accepted by you, then all that will be left in you will be a pulp of perception and opinion crush.

For instance, once, Mulla Nasruddin's wife drove home, got out of her car and promptly fell to the ground. Mulla rushed to her and asked, "What happened? Why did you faint? "She said, "It was too hot." He asked, "Why did you not open the windows?" She said, "What! Open the windows and let the neighbours know that our car is not air conditioned?" People are ready to die but they wouldn't like others to know their reality. It's a prestige issue that the car must be air conditioned, whether one can afford it or not. "She had to keep the windows closed".She may feel faint but she will suffer that ; to keep the windows open hurts much more!

Doing things to gratify others or to impress them would make you a stranger unto yourself masking your true nature. This would become a part of your blood and veins so much so, that at a certain point of time in your life, doing things for yourself would amaze you because all the while you were busy burning yourself to make others believe that you care for them. Repetitive attempts at this would breed in you the desire to be recognised for what you are doing, and thus losing the true spirit behind doing things.

## THE REAL YOU

*"There is a real inside which speaks and says: This is the real me!"*

— William James

Let me explain the above explanations further. I consider myself as an honest, frank person. I used to be brutally honest with people. As I interacted more and more with people, I realised that many couldn't handle my brutality and there was much of unpleasantness around. I received so much feedback asking me to change myself. I didn't change, I stopped being so brutal - the attitude of calling a spade a spade. I didn't give up on being an honest, frank person, but I am still working on my communication skills every day, learning to say the hard facts in a much better way. Besides my efforts to speak respectfully, if someone gets hurt because of my honesty, I seek forgiveness, but I am not willing to change the honest me for anyone or for anything. " What are my beliefs, what are the core principles with which I am navigating my life? What are my strengths/limitations? What are not my limitations but my nature? What makes me cry/happy? What do I want in life?" - contemplating on these, I feel I finally know an outline of the 'Real me'; at least, I am no longer a stranger to myself. It's liberating, it's truly liberating.

It's like a caterpillar that eventually metamorphosis into a beautiful butterfly. A caterpillar doesn't allow itself to be free from self. Whether it is through weakness or fear, a caterpillar must break free from what is holding it back by realising it can become a butterfly. A butterfly is free from the restraints of self. A butterfly has grown out from self and now seeks to love others with all the love it has while a caterpillar is still seeking to be loved by others. Unfortunately, many caterpillars do not know they have the ability to become butterflies and to remain in their cocoon until they die. So, come out of your cocoon and become butterfly you were always meant to become. Learn to know who you are by having a truly honest relationship with yourself. Grow out of any negativities that may be wedged with your mental and spiritual capacities. Having an original face means that you aren't dominated by any morality, religion, society, parents, teachers, priests or anyone. Yes, I have stopped explaining myself for, no amount of explanation will suffice for a person who doesn't understand me before the explanation. It's not egoistic confidence. It's just that something inside within me feels right, something inside me is simply at peace being me. Repetitive attempts at this would breed in you desire to be recognised for what you are doing and thus losing the spirit behind doing things. Believe me, you don't need another to make you feel special when you know 'YOU ARE SPECIAL'.

## LOST IN THE OUTER CIRCLES BY FORGETTING YOUR WAY TO CORE

Do you know the real reason why we are stuck and moving in circles? It is because we subscribe to society's definition of standards and so-called happiness and don't listen to our hearts. It always starts right from our childhood. There is so much pressure - to be topper in every class, to be an all-rounder, to be good in sports, in music, in literature and in science, to have the trendiest phone, to be most popular in high school, to be accepted in a group, to be liked by everyone, to be presentable, to get a degree that looks good, to go to the right college, to get the highest salary package, to be best and most faithful servant to a company, to get stressed out over the pressure of a competitive exam for which you had no interest in the first place, to be the best cook to impress the in-laws, to get slim just because it's fashionable, to make green tea your favourite drink, to like pizza because it is fashionable... There are countless examples and we all are or were a part of this maze at some point in our life. Even there are many more reasons why we keep straying towards the outer circle. People call it by different names, but we rationalise by always using the prefix 'better'— like better house, better salary, better company, better mainstream career, better acknowledgement, better acceptance, brand name, better respect, better tag, better position etc. We all have our reasons to not accept what we are doing. We succumb to the pressure of thinking that maybe it is not as good as 'others 'think it is.

Out of 100 things you do in life, do 80 things for the happiness of your loved ones.... At least 20 things do it for yourself. For these 20 things, write your own script; create your own definitions; make your own checklist. You have a right to fight. This earth and life is yours too. Ironically, when you commit to "It is better to earn a bad name and live a good life," you end up living a good life and also earning a good name. Let the limitations of other people not limit us. At every opportunity, let us get ahead of people and not get even with them. You have to achieve your goals while living amongst them. Don't waste your energy trying to live up to what somebody else wants you to be. Successful people win because they love what they do. Life is a state of consciousness. "As a man thinks in his heart, so is he". What we believe to be true about our environment and ourselves is derived from our core beliefs, which is the most predictor of all happiness and success. Let's just take a pledge today that we will fight for what we are and not get lost in bettering ourselves for the sake of society. Let's make a promise to ourselves to follow our hearts and find true happiness. That's all we need. Nothing else.

Cherish, adore, love yourself. Believe me, you don't need another to make you feel special when you know 'YOU ARE SPECIAL'. The world's a great place to live in when we are original, not copies of anything. It does not matter whether one copies Buddha, Krishna or Jesus—a copy is a copy. It is beneath human dignity to copy. Be original. Be your own master.

*"Listen to your being. It is continuously giving you hints; it is a still small voice. It does not shout at you. And if you are a little silent, you will start feeling your way. Be the person you are. Never try to be another, and you will become mature. Maturity is accepting the responsibility of being oneself—that's what maturity is all about."*

— *OSHO*

## LIVE BEFORE YOU LEAVE

*"Live life before it leaves you".*

— *Agothe Smyth*

We all know life is short. But how many of us live life to fullest. Have you ever put on quest to be more and do more, experienced the feeling that you were going backward? We all seem to be over-stretching ourselves. I am always saying, "I never thought life would be this busy". Could all this busyness actually prevent us or be creating blocks in our lives to what we are truly seeking? Could we actually start slowing down and asking yourselves different questions that would end up creating a more profound awareness in our lives? Can this hectic life with so many distractions keep us from a life where we are in appreciation of each and every moment of our day? We live in a world with so many expectations and so much to accomplish. Financial well-being, relationship that work, looking good and to be everything society wants us to be. All these burdens and expectations are like trying to push a bowling ball up a hill. Can we actually be causing damage to our well- being, to the physical mind and body and in turn slowly the real growth. We pursue all these things to create a place of wholeness. We seek a life that is complete and whole and dream of enjoying all that life has to offer. But do we ever get to the place of peace, calmness and serenity and do we ever find the love for our lives? We are doing one task and thinking about the next task. We never take time to be in the moment for just that.

We are in our cars, talking on phone and thinking about the meeting we have later that day. We pick up a friend from the airport and we just have to answer that call from a friend who just want to chit chat. How many of us rush blindly through our days, fall into bed exhausted, and wake up in next morning to do it over again? For many of us, our lives are composed of millions of meaningful moments, all strung together— perhaps with a sprinkling of sacred moments mixed in. I am sure you cannot think of a new sacred moment in your own life. Life taking to read a book, just sitting there viewing your balcony garden, and listening to your child, without all the noise going on your head of what you have to do next? Have you ever embarked an experience of dying while living in present moment? Last month I stumbled upon a video that focused on 'How to live life to the fullest? And there was an interesting exercise that the listeners were asked to try on themselves. Here is how it flows — sit somewhere in peace and imagine yourself dying. And focus on the thoughts that flow in your mind. Although it sounds unnatural and pessimistic, I went through this exercise. Initially I felt vulnerable, helpless, threatened, scared and hollow. Once I cross the boundary of initial reluctance, I felt very calm and had a short memory jog into my life so far... How I grew up, my parents, my loved ones and life in general.

Surprisingly, what actually popped up in my mind was what others did for me... A sense overwhelming gratitude filled me... How much I have been loved and how many opportunity life has provided me to share with others... Fights with the boss or loved ones did not even enter my mind like a soap bubble! All those things that I have attempted but desired for, flashed as a lightning in my mind. I felt an urgent need to fulfil all these desires. I felt this are the most important things that need to be done without any further delay. I must confess that these thoughts made me incomplete and thoughtfully morose for next few days. Yet, they somehow unlocked a door within me that was always closed. I learnt three valuable lessons from this experiment.

1. It made me realise, how easy it should be to love someone. For it makes you understand that we are here for a short span of time. All we have to do is find something good in a person; everyone indeed has something good within them. The problem with most of us is that we can easily identify the negatives; however, we don't make enough effort in identifying the positives. Once we start doing that, our lives become simpler. We feel so happy once start spreading love. Love is the energy that helps us to heal, whether we give this love to ourselves, or we receive it from another. Fill yourself with so much love that you have enough to share! The universe is ready to give you more, once you start giving more.
2. What you need to do next is to leave your past. For past is gone. And ahead lies a beautiful future. We are the only animals on earth who are always worried about the future. We are so busy thinking about our future that we something forgot to live our present, and when we realise our mistake, it may be too late because that present might have already become our past, which we can't get back at any cost

    I remember a story about a king who thought that he was suffering from a chronic disease. He used to call apothecaries from different places and when they pronounced that he was completely fine, he beheaded them. The king announced a huge reward for the person who could diagnose his illness. Hearing this, a quack came to the king and told him that the king was suffering from a chronic disease and the only panacea was to wear a happy man's shirt for one day. Hence the king's men were sent to find such a person but they found no one like that as each person experienced sadness for one thing or another. Finally, when his men were returning to the palace, they found a man rolling on the ground and laughing. When the king's men asked him the reason for his happiness, he told them that he was happy because he didn't have any possessions of his own so he didn't have the fear of losing anything. Just like this story, some of us are like the king who is under the influence of something which does not even exist or we are under the fear of losing something dear to us. But, none of us are interested in living life like the man in the story who had no possessions. We always want our life to go the way we want, no matter how much our way of living may hurt others, and when things go the way they must go, we say 'Our life is hell'. We must change the way we look at our life not the way life looks at us. Life would be so boring if everything went the way we wanted it to. It is when things go the other way that life will appear to be something worth living. Our outlook to life must be that "my life is a roller coaster ride and I am going to enjoy all the ups and downs to the fullest till it comes to an end on its own". Thus, life expects you to stop looking back; life wants you to embrace this given moment. Because each moment you live is precious. Those moments will not come back again.

3. Thirdly, being in that moment. How about just being? I sometimes take a Friday afternoon off from work and other chores and just be with the day — enjoying the sunshine and warmth of sun as it kisses my forehead. Do you ever slow down and listen to birds sing, or watch a humming bird hover like a helicopter as it pecks at a bougainvillea? Do you still feel the coolness and that little tickle of the

grass on your feet or are you just traversing this earth in pursuit of something you just can't get your hands around? Also try in breathing in and out slowly and feel the air move through your body. Do it now! Appreciate this moment and be in gratitude for this moment. Yes, you can tend to your busy life later, but from time to time stop and just BE. Be open seeing and feeling what is going around you and really appreciate the moment for whatever it offers. Let the world take care of itself for a while. You don't have to fix everything. Why do we wait for major events to honour these sacred moments? Why can't everyday be sacred? Each moment? Every moment is sacred, if we decide, to make it that way. Honouring the sacred means simply choosing to make each moment count. How do we change our perception to one of sacredness? What does it mean to stay in the present moment? Let's use an example: When most of us washes dishes, we hurry through it, often thinking about the million other things we need to get done that day (or the next day). Our minds are scattered all over the place, focusing on everything but not on the present task. Washing dishes is not the most exciting experience. However, if we choose to make it a sacred experience, we want to focus it. We want to take our time and pay attention to how the water feels our hands, how the soap cleanses away the grease and grime, and the sense of satisfaction we get as each dish moves from the dirty pile on to the strainer, now clean and shiny. May be that still doesn't sound very thrilling. As we give our full attention to washing the dishes, we are not only doing, we are being. In those moments, we are fully alive and conscious. Those moments will not come back again and the decision and things we do in every moment create reality. You can tend to your busy life later, but from time to time stop and just BE.

4. Lastly, never give up your passions. NEVER. Yes, it might be difficult to follow your dreams. But remember, when you have a passion within you, you can stretch yourself infinitely. Then it is God within you saying, 'You are made for this' You will perform wonders, keep going. Take tiny steps. You have to cross the milestone. Just don't stop. Choosing the right one is tricky. You have to stay guided and follow your intuition. Because intuition plays an important role in your life. Never suppress your intuitions; they are guiding you to make right choice. The road ahead may be long. It might be endless. Yet, you have to keep yourself motivated. For the rocky roads lead to beautiful destinations You choose your own road. You create your own path. Embrace the setbacks.

Love yourself more when you slip off the road, when you get lost. Because you tried. Smile. And stand again. But keep going. For life is short and your passion is big. LIVE this moment. Breathe in this air. Smile even if something goes wrong. For that is preparing you for next moment. When things go your way, it is called LIVING, but when things go their own way, it is called LIFE. So Live to the Fullest. Before you leave.

## LIFT YOURSELF BY YOURSELF

*"If you want to lift yourself up lift up someone else."*

— *Booker T. Washington*

I saw a bumper sticker proclaiming, "Dude, don't follow me — I am following my bliss." Good decision. 'Limitlessness 'like an ocean is the only way to define human potential. How much more creative and successful would your life be if you remained true to your own inner guidance rather than imitating the paths chosen by others. Numerous evolved souls have walked the planet earth. Buddha, Mahavira, Dalai Lama, Vivekananda, Chinmayananda, Mahatma — giving us their teachings, values and doctrines thereby guiding us to live a holistically abundant life. Yet, we all still have our own struggles and challenges to live life with heightened awareness and consciousnesses. Why? Are the teachings, the preachings and the doctrines inadequate, incomprehensible or not implementable? Think about it— why are we still struggling in life. All emotions like worry, lust, discontent, jealousy, fear, ego, attention, are purely because we find a connection between independent thought and create a concept for ourselves and start relating with that concept, we create an imaginary shaft with our thoughts and we suffer because of this. We start feeling burdened. Thus, we need so many evolved souls and masters to guide us. Is one doctrine, one path or one way not enough for the entire humanity to evolve? Yes, I found answers in the quote from the 'Upanishad', which state— *"Lift yourself by yourself."*

## WILLINGNESS TO CHANGE YOURSELF

It doesn't matter what path you follow, which doctrine or value systems you imbibe; at the end of the day nothing changes, if you don't change. Everything changes when you change. If you have to achieve what you haven't achieved before, then you must be willing to do what you have never done before. That simply means you must change. You have a shell, a tendency to remain as you are. You don't grow. You refuse to throw away your lower values and petty habits! But evolution is the innermost desire of the 'inner self'. Nature is a shining example of the hidden powers in the Universe. A tiny seed of banyan tree is very well protected as long as it remains a seed. There is a security in remaining a seed. To sprout into a tree makes the seed susceptible. But then, what else is the purpose of seed? The seed contains infinite forests within it. And only in becoming an extremely huge and big banyan tree, those possibilities are possible. In order to embrace security, we resist changes and in resisting change, we stagnate. We build our own comfort zones and create a prison out of it. Hence, become prisoners in it. The important quality of great people is their willingness to change. And for that, they grow. That which does not change, does not grow and it dies. Give up who you are, so that you can become what you can be. Discover a new you within you. We can even be handpicked by the evolved soul yet — only we can do what we need to do to improve our life. Doing cannot be delegated. And unless we do change ourselves, our world remains the same.

## CHECK YOUR MOTIVATION

While most of us go through life crippled by fear and laziness, only some boldly unlock the power of right motivation with themselves. We have suffered so much by the slings and arrows of treacherous fate, broken relationships and poor health that we become a depressed lot. We live like robots, going from one society to another, mindlessly and unquestioningly going to college, getting a job, lusting for promotions and power, getting married, bringing up children, hanging out with friends, food gatherings,addiction to fight boredom, taking the old vacation, bearing the pain of old age and separation from children and relatives and ultimately meeting death. We don't have the energy or motivation to break the mould and look outside our small selves to serve a large cause, open our hearts and love others. We always worried about tomorrow and have subconsciously blocked our dynamic will and loving hearts. Our nature is love but we have stopped loving and living. But motivation can be expressed in humble measures and yet bring about powerful change. Moreover, it can benefit even the simplest of souls. True motivation gently pushes us to love, be happy, to accept whatever comes our way with equanimity and unconsciously learn to be actively calm in unfavourable situations and never hurt or cheat others. It encourages us to try and reach out to others and alleviate their pain even at the height of our suffering; for it is forgetting our small selves that we surmount all misery and diseases and find happiness and drive to live. Take small steps and be motivated to do something for someone else. Trust me, you won't regret it! Everyone around you will notice a change in your aura and feel encouraged to pay it forward. So, motivation is an inside-out phenomenon to make others life more purposeful and blessed.

## RISE ABOVE THE CHECKLIST

Each one of you have been given a social checklist and strict adherence is expected. Everybody follows it. Then, why should you rebel about it? Even a slight deviation from the checklist, you will be called selfish. It will create hullabaloo. Having decided to embark on your own path, one's first task is to "Lift yourself by yourself." Wake up! Wake up! Freedom is not given. It must be taken. Rise against all odds. The entire significance of a kite's freedom comes from it being disciplined by the thumb and a finger that is holding the string let go it, the kite will fall into a directionless death. The kite does not rise with the wind, but against the wind. Sometimes to the right, sometimes to the left, sometimes upwards, and sometimes it has to fall to rise... finally itself up in the skies. Life is never going to be free from hindrances. You will have to lift yourself by yourself. You live only once. This is the only chance you have got to be 'you'. Please don't miss yourself. Rise above the checklist. Expand the definition of your life. Live above the average. Let your life be a message to the next generation. When we have become free, we need not go mad and throw away society and rush off to die in the forest or cave; we shall remain where we were, only we shall understand the whole thing. The same phenomena will remain, but with a new meaning. We do not know the world yet; it is only through the freedom that we see what it is, and understand its nature.

Even the epitome of compassion, Lord Mahavira professed, *"Live and let live"* and not "Let live and live." After all, if you don't know to live, then how are you going to help others to live. The messiah of love, Jesus Christ, also put you ahead by stating, *"Love thy neighbour as you love yourself."*

## SELF OBSERVATION

Move from focusing on which path to follow or which religion to imbibe because all methods work if you are willing to work on yourself. Start by observing yourself and your life. Instead of being a vagabond and a mere collector of knowledge, focus on building experiences which will turn knowledge into wisdom. Knowledge can be handed over to you; wisdom is self-created by turning all knowledge learnt into a useful experience. Knowledge, when applied at the appropriate moment, turns into wisdom and it is entirely in our hands. In the game of pole vaulting, the player uses a long flexible pole as aid to jump over a bar. Every pole vaulter knows that they need the pole to take off and gain the elevation and at the appropriate moment, the pole must be dropped to cross the bar. We all need to be pole vaulters in life. Through the evolved souls and their teachings (our pole), we gain the elevation we need in life. If at the elevation, we become mere spectators, be sure we will fall, as the pole will not hold us elevated forever. Using this elevation of evolved souls one can be successful. In other words, success comes only to those who apply the teachings (the knowledge gained) and transform it into wisdom to cross every hurdle they face.

In short, lift yourself by yourself. Then, how do the teachings, the doctrines, the path help me? We all understand the need of a compass while navigating, right? These value systems and doctrines make the navigation easy. Just like how Google maps help us find locations with ease, every path helps us and guides us in our journey of self-discovery. In the interior of every being lies a compelling urge for change, for growth into a richer and deeper state of existence. The urge for evolution in human beings stems from a wish to be free of the sense of limitation and imperfection.

The process by which the human mind breaks free of its fetters to expand into a vaster dimension of consciousness is called Self-discovery. Stand up for yourself. Let the push come within. The world will stand by you.

Chapter 13

MAKE YOURSELF COUNT

## MAKE YOURSELF COUNT

*"Above all else, I had learned the one thing every person has to learn to make it through life: the only person you can truly count is yourself."*

— *C.J Roberts*

When was the last time you stole a moment for yourself? It's rather difficult for us to indulge in something purely for ourselves because as a society, we seem wired for guilt. Guilt about spending on a new pair of shoes when the money could've been — spent on groceries for the week, guilt about allowing ourselves to watch a late-night show because the kids needs us back home... It seems — anything that gives us pure pleasure is a complete no-no because some or the other responsibilities has always to be fulfilled. For the jet setters, getting time with oneself is a luxury and often an impossibility.

The 'I' movement has stirred the world. Everyone is asking - have you taken your 'Vitamin 'I' for the day? It's a moment of the day you keep for 'I, me, myself'. It's about booking that lone chair in a restaurant and relishing noodles all by yourself, or buying a bouquet of yellow roses for your eyes only. But are you part of this movement? Can you recollect the last time you pampered yourself? Because of the growing consumerism, everyone wants everything and very soon. In this mad rush no one has any time left for them! Life has become materialistic and mechanical. Now the focus is what I am going to get out of this? Also, we are not leaving any room to err. We are perpetually trying to be perfect. Look around you— busy professionals, stressed home maker, corporate honchos — do they really have time for themselves? It is this pressure which that is driving our lives.

The 'living for yourself' isn't just a vast psychological experiment. It is spending some qualitative time with oneself, doing something that gives us creative satisfaction builds our self-confidence and self-respect, two very important attributes for self-growth. Moreover, self-reliance is nothing but ability and desire to provide for oneself. It means to accept responsibility for your own happiness and sorrows, your actions and afflictions. Indeed, for your life. Why does this appear so hard? Why do we look outside of us, to friends, family, neighbours, everywhere but ourselves, for emotional and physical sustenance?

This is because of the patterns imbibed in childhood. As children we observe that we need to 'earn' affection, that love is always conditional, that it requires being manipulative. We begin to believe that unconditional love is non-existent or that no matter how hard we try; we are undeserving of it. These patterns are carried into adulthood and we learn to treat ourselves the same way; we berate ourselves, mistrust ourselves, we continue as motherless children, wrapped in self-pity and rejection of ourselves.

## ON YOUR OWN

*"Give your life to a cause greater than yourself.......*

*make it happen make it count!"*

*— Kelly Swanson*

When we accept responsibility for our actions, some beautiful thing happens. Life is no longer a chore or about passing the buck. Responsibility means we don't want any part in the blame game, duties become apparent, we do what we have to do. We are so tune with ourselves and our real needs that we only take what is essential. There is no insecurity, therefore no greed or hoarding, either materially or emotionally.

Our greatest shining example of this is Mahatma Gandhi, the very paragon of self-reliance. Gandhiji's concepts of Swaraj and Swadeshi translate as independence and self-sufficiency or self-reliance. Swaraj or self-rule is the only expression of the intrinsic truth of the individual. It does not deny one's inter-connectedness with others, but ensures that one can take care of oneself first, then one's family, loved ones, and rest of the world. Gandhiji learned how to do most of his work himself, including washing, ironing and cutting his own hair. No work was too big or small. He cleaned toilets, cleaning up after himself and others. He learned and taught how to build homes, run a printing press, publish a newspaper. While in jail in South Africa, he learned how to make leather slippers.

Self-reliance, as recommended by Gandhiji, is one of the master-virtue in which several virtues reinforce and support each other. When I am self-reliant, I am a law unto myself, the knowledge of right and wrong springs from me. I rely on myself to administer my own morality. I am discipline, I am trust. I am happiness. I am truth incarnate. When we see this, we realise life and its joys and sorrows are only part of creation. All life and relations then, we realise, are role play. We learn to make concessions for others, become more accommodating of their flaws and less judgmental. We become less insecure, more tolerant. Individualise yourself. Don't get lost in the crowd. Do extraordinary things to make yourself great.

## COUNT ON YOURSELF

*"You have to count on living every single day in a way you believe will make you feel good about your life — so that if it were over tomorrow, you'd be content with yourself."*

— *Jane Seymour*

A real value of our lives is in how we use our time as we journey from womb to tomb. Calamities that befall us, hardships and obstacles one encounters on the road, are positive blessings. They knit the muscles more firmly and teach self-reliance.

Divya Bhandara, now 47 yrs of age, was born with a severe hearing impairment. But her mother Reena, ex-principal of Hellen Keller Institute for the deaf-blind, recalls the brightness of her spirit as a child: "It took a lot to get Divya down, even her deafness couldn't. She was enthusiastic one, always up for a game of football or cricket with the boys."

Divya, even today, has no qualms about approaching people with a bright smile and handing them her business card for Divya Soft Toys, her brave foray into self-reliance and economic independence. Being a handicapped youngster in India brought its share of discouragement. Despite half-baked government policies on reservation of seats, scarcity of jobs for disabled individuals, she kept herself occupied doing various short beautician and home science courses, developing her other skills rather than dwelling on her handicap. This has helped her circumvent a lot of heartbreak and self-doubt. Her small enterprise keeps her happily occupied. During the slow months she plans for the busy season or holds exhibitions. Today, she's a driven entrepreneur, learning from her mistakes and keen on improving business.

## MAKE TODAY COUNT

*"Making each day count like it's your last day to fulfil your dreams, is unarguably the master key to a future full of great rewards."*

— *Edmond Mbiaka*

Seize the present moment and success will be yours. I strongly believe that today is the best day and this hour is the dearest, and this moment is the decider. When I take care of this moment, the oncoming moment will pave the way for new; hence I strongly believe that every moment counts. So, make yourself bigger than your words and action. When I don't make use of this moment, I know I am postponing the progress to my own victory. It is like how mere seeds can't become trees unless planted in the right soil at the right time. In the journey of life waves of opportunities keep coming but whoever decides to make use of those waves by putting in the maximum efforts, alone can test the fruits of victory. Remember unless you grab the opportunities with both the hands and make use of them in right sense, you can never stand on the victory stand. Hence it is paramount to register strongly that 'today' is the winning day. I will never get it again and if I believe only in tomorrow, the victory is only a distance. With a firm resolution tell yourself that today is the day! this the opportunity and I will give the best. I adhere to this strongly and advocate it to others as well. Beautify your today, you can achieve what you never thought possible...

## COUNT YOUR BLESSINGS

*"Count your blessings. Once you realise how valuable you are and how much you have going for you, the smiles will return, the sun will break out, the music will play, and you will be able to move forward the life that God intended for you with grace, strength, courage and confidence."*

— Og Mandingo

So many times, a door in life closes and we become angry, cursing our fate. We lose a job, our girlfriend or boyfriend leaves us, our house is virtually destroyed in flood and we have to move.

The famous Roman orator, Cicero, who lived in the first century AD, had this to say about attitude of gratitude, *"A thankful heart is not only the greatest Virtue, but the parent of all virtues"*. At first glance, this is a puzzling one, but Cicero is probably one of the world's first motivational speakers, perhaps it is worth taking seriously. Still, we must ask, what is a thankful heart, especially in a world where hearts are so easily broken, where calamities and disappointments for so many lurks behind every corner and where life seems so easily to dispense failure and dissatisfaction and failure?

It would seem that a thankful heart is possessed by a man or a woman who habitually looks at the world with a feeling of thanksgiving or gratitude despite what other people might think of the world about them. To obtain a thankful heart, one must either be slightly insane, given the nature of things, or have adopted an attitude of thankfulness, despite the normal course of things for some over-riding experiences.

Things that seem bad are always the worst possible things. Sometimes they are just a way of the universe opening up new possibilities for you to enjoy. Thus, at the very least, when something unexpected happens, you can realise that you are stepping into the unknown. But is there a way you can step into this unknown and perhaps seemingly dangerous waters and still put your best foot forward? Perhaps, you can use the healing and strengthening power of gratitude. 'Gratitude is not an emotion', but a power that empowers you to move forward in life.

But, instead, of letting our gratitude be like the backdrop of painting a colourful but distant background to the events and drama in our lives. So, thanksgiving or attitude of gratitude should be a very positive prominent part of our lives. How should we do this?

"Every moment of every morning of every sunrise of every day is always special". Simply put, "Every moment of life is special", for it holds within the power to make someone special. I open my eyes to the wake-up call and I raise my hands in gratitude. "Everyone has not got this day, but I have. Thank you, my Lord, I will make the most of it". "I wear a jogging gear and as I am leaving, I pray. Everyone may not get this chance to take care of his health and be fit. I have got it. Let me make the most of it." Ever since I have realised the blessings of all beautiful people and experiences in my life, I not only feel blessed but have also started cherishing their presence in my life a lot more. I just merge into experience with them and made the most of every moment. And it goes on and on and till the last moment of the day as I slowly move in my bed before closing my eyes and stating, "Everyone will not go to sleep peacefully, but I do because I live my life in gratitude and gratitude annihilates all form of disturbances In gratitude, I realised how much I have, in gratitude, I have found peace. The more I am grateful, the more I have been receiving from life. Gratitude is the way to both peace and prosperity. Gratitude is a result of realising. Everyone doesn't get everything in life. So, when you have it, make the most of it". The real secret, however; is be thankful for all the wonderful things you have in your life and to always seek the hidden advantage in the events that surround you. Dare to dream and make those dreams into your reality through your action and thoughts.

## Chapter 14
# NATURE NURTURES SELF

# NATURE NURTURES SELF

> *"To capture beauty*
>
> *with nature,*
>
> *is like nurture self"*
>
> — *Been A Mystic*

Nature can be your secret remedy, your manna, your instant restoration, soothing your frazzled mind and opening doors to creativity. Being outside in nature inspires feelings of awe and wonder and acquaints us with our higher self. Nature is the mother of mothers. God manifests. In every movement and manifestation of her myriad life forms and forces, she conveys a teaching-sometimes powerful and vibrant, sometimes subtle and silent, sometimes ruthless and terrifying. She shows us through her own unsurpassable integrity, beauty and being, the states of mind and attitude we must adopt if we wish to attain self-realisation. She is the enlightened state, pure and natural, it is this that she coaxes us to recognise, in her infinitely patient, infinitely relative, way.

## NATURE EMBODIES THE INNER PRINCIPLE

How completely in the moment she is, how still and free holding on to nothing! There is no ego operating. In spite of the fact the trees can't move, they are happily dancing. Observe the flowers, though they know their life is short, they never forget to spread their fragrance all around. Nature teaches through the smallest life experience. What really moves is the sight of autumn leaves falling. They depart with no drama, so cheerfully. When they live, they do so with no sense of achievement or vanity. With equal grace they exist. She is awe of the complete contentment manifest in nature. It is this that makes you feel peaceful in her presence. We have abused our mind, the less the intelligence. You can stand in wonderment and awe at nature's intelligence. And we are part of that. When we recognise that, the ego crumbles. Always nature teach us how to attain success in a harmonious way. For instance, when fresh leaves grow from a stalk, it does not hinder the fall of sunlight on the other leaves. It fills in between instead. Or look at the flowers in a hedge. Each fresh flower will fill gap, instead of taking the place already occupied. They will never push and shove the way we do in the local train. There is a great co-operation in nature. Look at the big trees in a jungle. During monsoons they absorb a great amount of water in their roots, which they release later during the dry climes, thereby allowing plants and shrubs to thrive. There harmony is fantastic! Perm Nirmal, an electronics engineer, entrepreneur and workshop trainer, is equally responsive to nature's teachings. He adds, *"I learnt to use my intuition from nature. Every time I get stuck in a technological problem, I spend time alone with nature and look for signals. The logical mind cannot go beyond the direction of reason. If you look at how creativity manifests in nature, you will first see an aura of what is to come and then the actual fruit or flower. It is equivalent of the meditative mind".*

Nirmal uses the wisdom manifest in nature to help him solve the most pragmatic of problems such as investment decisions. He says, *"I had a sum for investment but I was unsure of how to invest it. When I looked for signals from nature, I kept seeing yellow flowers. So, I invested in gold and made a lot of money soon after."* His brushes with nature have not always been quite so benign. He recalls riding a motorcycle one late night in the forest area adjoining his home, and coming across a panther about to cross road. He says, 'There was no fear, we were both creatures of nature with no intention of harming each other. The panther went its way and I went mine. He really understood the meaning of the term 'kinship with nature' for the first time. Nirmal also conducts nature camps where he invites corporates to unwind and sit at the lotus feet of Mother Nature. Not just this. Nature impacts various parts of the brain in a positive manner has been proved in various countries. Here is an excerpt from the article Nature Nurture Creativity, from News Centre, University of Utah. Backpackers scored 50 per cent better on a creativity test after spending four days in nature, disconnected from electronic devises, according to a study by psychologists from the University of Utah and the University of Kansas.

## NATURE — A COSTLESS LUXURY

*"It's not nature verses nurture. It's nurturing your nature."*

*— Andrew Solomon*

To lie down on the carpet of grass, to sleep in the open air, a lonely stroll, to wander on the beach with a loved one, there is nothing beautiful than the way the ocean refuses to stop kissing the seashore line no matter how many times it is sent away. To sit beside the waves of the sea, the smell of a fragment garden, the night skies, in the silence of forest we can learn so many truths! We can hear and feel the night life with the sounds of insects, the grunts of animals, birds flapping, swaying trees, the rustle of the bushes and the occasional hoot of an owl or a forest fowl during a night safari into a thick forest. Being with Nature humbles you. When you stand in front of a huge mountain, you see how much more there is to life than just you. Nature gives so many free joys, like air and water and its sheer beauty. Another beauty is a dewdrop dancing on a blade of grass, marvel lung at a sunrise, dancing in the rain. Golden moments and memorable experiences are at every man's disposal. They can't be given to you. You need to gift them unto yourself. Thus, nature is one of the costless luxuries. A gift by the self to the self for the self. Never miss out the above costless luxury and each one of us can experience from this bountiful gift called life.

## NATURE AND ME, AN INTIMATE..

I have often wondered at the singularity vs duality of nature and myself. How we are both connected / one or how are we both apart / different? Very often, I simply draw my energy from nature — the soothing balm to my spirit, the spa for my weary body, the relaxant for my overworked mind. Mostly I find her giving, even if I ask for nothing. There are fleeting moments when I experience my oneness with her and me. Standing under a tree in a rain shower, my arms outstretched, my face upturned to skies. I've experienced the oneness. In the melting moment of a sunset, where the earth dissolves into experiencing the grand dance of the setting sun, the ochres, the purples romancing her like a lover. A tiny violet wild flower can give me as much pleasure as a clean sandy shore kissed by a pristine ocean for miles. For me, it is a force which gives me life. My goal is to make my mind like the sky, which reflects the electric storms and returns to serenity. "My plants are dearer to me than anything else. I plant them tend to tender little saplings and in sixty days, they bloom!" I feel so happy. I sit alone and enjoy those flowers, being with them is deeply relaxing. I feel more connected to nature, which is the supreme power. My mental health gets a big positive dose and many negative forces are taken away. Often, my flowers act as a psychological guide. They give me the energy to care for them even when I am tired. There is so much attachment and sometimes my flowers talk to me. Once on a task, I hurried past my collection of flower pots in the sunlit balcony. Just as I was about to open the door and leave, a fragrance came creeping towards me as if calling me. I turned back and with surprise realised that five beautiful pearly jasmine flowers laden with beautiful fragrance of their first blooming, were waiting to greet me! They internally called me to look at them. This is the magical bond between me and my flowers. If someone gardening with their own hands, plants will always respond to them, their touch. Today, I felt my secret out. People often asks me, "What keeps you smiling, what gives you ability to find joy in small things, what bestows this childlike wonder in you?" Apart from my physical and emotional needs, and sometimes not even those, nature is my go-to. "Nature is God and God is nature. Nature has unconditionally taken responsibility to nurture, protect, uplift, share with and care for us. I don't look for anything other than nature". Do not look at yourself with disgust, you are a gift to this earth. You are beautiful, you are a light, an energy, an essence. You are nature herself. Punctuate your life with costless luxury called "Nature".

## Chapter 15
# OCEAN AND I

# OCEAN AND I

*"The ocean makes me feel really small and it makes me put my whole life into perspective — it humbles you and makes you almost like you've been baptised. I feel born again when I get out of the ocean."*

— Beyonce' Knowles

## LEARNING FROM THE OCEAN...

Life is how you see it. It's not about what you are told, it is about how you face it. We like the people who are like rivers and lakes — calm, stable and peaceful. They are confined, they always know what they want to do in life and so, they are predictable. Rivers are so calm that you can actually see your image on its surface. We all like people like that, who can be our mirrors and guide us. But one thing we don't realise that rivers are confined within boundaries. They have a limit. They can flow only in between their banks.

Once I was told that I am not calm and composed, that I should be like a river— calm and peaceful. This comment triggered a sequence of infinite thoughts within me. Well, whatever was said was unimpeachable truth. Yes, I agree I am not calm and composed like a river. That is because I AM AN OCEAN! An Ocean which is way beyond stability. I am an ocean unpredictability wild, unstable and, most importantly, limitless. I cannot be confined. And here lies my strength and uniqueness.

An Ocean cannot form reflections because it is busy in reflecting its own beauty formed by the rays of the sun falling on its dancing waves. So am I not here to show others what they are; I am here to be the next, better version of myself! Therefore I am busy creating my own version. The ocean has a never-say attitude. Every coming wave goes back and yet there is another wave. The ocean never stops. These unstoppable waves have been smothered several sharp rocks on the shore. So, the ocean teaches us that with persistence you can change anything - any old habit, behaviour... whatever. And these clashing waves are music itself, becoming a therapy for healing. Be happy if you are inquisitive about things happening around you. Don't let it upset you if you cannot fit into the box and find yourself standing apart. If you are sensitive and get overwhelmed by even the smallest act, think of it as blessings and not a punishment. Because only such limitless people can unveil infinite possibilities. Our sensitivity will open up new ways to restore faith in humanity. I am unstable as a wave of emotions is always flowing through me. I am here to feel everything around me. The budding flower, the creation of a new leaf, the birth of a puppy, the tree shading all leaves to decorate itself with a new look, dewdrops shining like pearls on a leaf, the innocence of children. I just want to feel everything. I find magic in every creation of God. I get overwhelmed by even the smallest act. This makes me unstable but the law of nature states that only wavy, unstable ocean can make pearls. That's the beauty of ocean. Oceans may appear unstable on the surface but deep within they are meditative.

The ocean is a dwelling to infinite species of different genres. It serves as a mother to all. Like the ocean, I am mother at heart. It does not matter to me whether it is a human being, a dog, a cat or anything else. All I understand is that it's a child in need of a mother. And a mother does not belong to any species. For a mother, the child is a unique gift of God. To me all are creations of God. Loving oneself deeply, completely and thoroughly would unfold his or her nature and radiate serene love. Love is the journey from within and without. Until we learn to embrace ourselves, there is no way we can be loved and also love others. Love is respecting every soul we come across. In rejoicing in the Creator's creation, we ascend to loving the Creator. Be proud and say 'YES I AM AN OCEAN'. And it is nature's law that finally all rivers, lakes and streams merge into the ocean.

# Chapter 16
# PUTTING YOURSELF FIRST IS NOT SELFISH

# PUTTING YOURSELF FIRST IS NOT SELFISH

*"Putting yourself first is not selfish. Quite the opposite. You must put your happiness and health first before you can be of help to anyone else"*

— *Simon Sinek*

First and foremost, people feel guilty and selfish due to their misconception of what the term "putting yourself first" means. Putting yourself doesn't mean that the other people are not important. It just means you prioritise yourself over other. There is an order in which you serve. When you wake up in the morning to serve your needs before you serve others. My mornings are mostly easy without any rush as that is the most important time of our day. I sit in the balcony, which overlooks a beautiful tree blooming with flowers, look at the rising sun, and pray to the Almighty to energise me to make me strong. Then I meditate for half an hour so that I can transfer my energy to all people who come in contact with me and help them to become strong. Prioritisation isn't about how important a person is to you; it's more about the order of operation. It is crucial because you can't please everyone at the same time. You can only give your undivided attention to one person or one task at a time. So, we have to choose wisely, prioritising the most effective person to serve is none other than ourselves.

## "PUTTING YOURSELF FIRST" IS THE BEST GIFT YOU CAN GIVE TO THE WORLD

You have to take care of yourself. The more you "Put Yourself first" the more you're about to serve. It benefits everyone and everything else too. When you are healthy, reduces the burden of your spouse and your family to take care of you. As you are more energetic and nourished you can also contribute better than usual. People around you don't get hurt by your occasional outbursts of anger, resentment, or stress. When you take care of your emotions, you can go a long way helping others to live happier, fuller life. If you learn to 'Love Yourself' you'll know how to actually love others.

## IS EXHAUSTING AND INEFFECTIVE OF "PUTTING OTHERS" AS THE PRIORITY?

Stifled by demands? Harassed by unrelenting demands on your time and energy, you may be in danger of losing the real plot— helping your own self. Yes, there are people who make unreasonable demands on your time and energy. You can never do enough for them - meet one demand and they are waiting with another few. Whether they are grateful or not is beside the point. You end up depleting reserves that you need for your own self. Everyone wants a piece of you, and worse, they do not feel they are doing anything wrong. Someone sends you a message, almost immediately followed by an email. As if that isn't enough, they follow it up with a call. This is followed by the most intrusive of all— stalking on WhatsApp to ensure you follow through with their demand. In this noise and chaos, where is the time for your own self? In their own heightened sense of entitlement, they forget to respect others needs and boundaries. The answer is— by making a virtue of much-maligned emotion of selfishness. We need to guard our private spaces and priorities with a fierce possessiveness. Not just charity, but goodness, love, kindness and all things nice begins at home with your own self too. What you can do for your own self, you cannot do effectively for the world. It would be the most foolish to lose the real plot by enmeshing yourself in the chaos of selfish demands from others. Develop some selfishness of your own. Identify your own needs and goals. Appropriate resources of time and energy you need to meet these. Keep aside time to meet people and refuse to do for the rest of the day. Learn to say a polite and firm 'no' to people who are perpetually feeding off you with no return. Refuse to be taken for granted by anyone, no matter how loved or close. Last and not least, understand that you cannot possibly help everyone. Do not try; it isn't healthy.

## WHY "PUTTING YOURSELF FIRST" REALLY WORTH IT?

I distinctly remember the incident that got me okay with the 'selfish' tag.

I had to meet a friend who had come to town just for a day. She wanted to meet me once her work got done, and I was busy in completing a creative project at that time. She requested that I reschedule, but I didn't, simply because I didn't want to. That was quite a selfish move, (something she told me later). However, the point was, I took a decision that was more comfortable for me, than for anyone else, and while, at that point, I did feel a little bad, I got over the feeling real fast. For the first time in my life, I felt that I am not cheating myself constantly. What a feeling it is to start becoming the original me as my Creator has created me to be. My opinion of myself, my day and my work are beginning to mean more to me than anybody else's words... It is really worth to 'putting yourself first' both personally and professionally.

## YOU CAN CHANGE YOURSELF

I remember reading somewhere that the concept of 'selfish' has got a lot of bad press. If you don't make the decisions that you feel are the best for you, who is going to? To turn these decisions over to someone else means that you will be doing what they think is best for you. The reality is that you cannot force yourself to change the decisions for someone else. You can change for yourself and take responsibility for yourself. It is not what happens to you in life that determines how you feel; it is how you respond to what happens. The only you, makes you feel anything is YOU. The fact is, you have complete control over only one thing-your mind. When you develop an internal locus of control, the external factor will neither sway you nor shall you keep the negative emotions alive by feeding them with thoughts and energy. And finally, ACTION is everything. Put the above ways to work and witness your journey of transformation.

## YOU HAVE TO TAKE CARE OF YOURSELF EVENTUALLY

You can heal yourself and pay attention to yourself and when you tend to take care of your own physical, mental, emotional needs first, you place yourself in the position to be actually 'selfless'. Not 'selfless' as a means of receiving the support you need (which is what it ends up being, most of the time).

Robert Pinto, a cocaine addict was on his way home after procuring his 'stuff' from his supplier on Shuklajee Street in Mumbai. It was the 1970s when drug addiction was still a remote American affliction. The cab broke down in front of Mt Carmel church in Bandra. Russel wandered in and sat awhile listening to an Irish priest deliver a sermon on repentance. It was Lent. The sermon urged everyone to repent for the sufferings they were causing loved ones and themselves. When Russel walked out of the church, he took the long road to self-recovery home. It took him two years to give up his dependent on drugs. While on the path he found succour in the Bible and teachings of Swami Vivekananda. Then in 1992, he set up Sevadhan, pioneering rehab center for substance abusers in Mumbai. Two years later, Russell died in a freak drowning accident in Baga, Goa. He left behind a young wife Clema and two children. Clema surrendered herself to the situation. And was amazed at the faith, hope, love and resilience she found with in herself. Later on, Clema went up to set up Nav Norman a rehab center in rural Thane and later Sahara, a half-way house for alcohol and substance abusers. The more you "Put Yourself first", the more you're to serve others. If you learn to Love Yourself, you'll know how to actually Love other people.

The world rejoices when you are at the best. By being the best version of yourself, you have more to offer and give the world. It's exhausting and ineffectively putting others as the priority. Energy transfers to the ones you love. Rather than showing up with an exhausted burnout self, you bring positive energy, compassion, and peace to the world. You inspire the people around you to do the same and be the best version of themselves. When you "Put Yourself First", you are not waiting for someone else to fill you up. You give because you are already in abundance of love and overflowing with love. Furthermore, it's only when you love yourself that you truly know how to love others.

# Chapter 17
# QUALITY CONSCIOUSNESS

# QUALITY CONSCIOUSNESS

*"Quality is never an accident; it is always the result of intelligent effort."*

— *John Ruskin*

Quality consciousness implies awareness of yourself and the environment around you— most importantly, YOU. Quality consciousness is that which has the highest degree of development of its own consciousness. That means that someone who is conscious of himself, can have different degrees, or levels of consciousness. It enhances the quality of decision making, the ability to inspire high levels of commitment, empathy and authenticity by bringing in love to the self-first.

## WHAT IS QUALITY CONSCIOUSNESS?

*"To get more out of yourself, you have to expect more out of yourself. Before your body can achieve it, your mind has to perceive it".*

—*Ricky Williams*

Quality consciousness is expecting more from yourself than anyone else expects of you. The only expectations you should live up are the ones you expect of yourself. Expect more from yourself, from life, and from everything you do. To accomplish more, you must expect more from yourself. High expectations may lead to disappointment, but they all lead to breakthroughs and life-changing results. Disappointments are a result of failed expectations. Don't think anyone can love you more than you can love yourself. And no one can understand you better than yourself. If you expect others to love you the way you want, then you will be hurt in the end... just be true to yourself and let your happiness be within you and not outside depending on the crowd. To have less disappointments, either expect less from other people or demand more from yourself.

*"Demand more from yourself than anyone else could ever expect".*

*— Tony Robbins*

Quality consciousness is setting higher standards for yourself than the world has set for you. Challenge yourself! Set the bar high and raise your standard to create positive change in life. Standards are things you set for yourself, by no longer putting up with less than what you are capable of doing. When you get in the groove of continuously setting new standards for things you tolerate in yourself, you will elevate your pattern of behaviour to higher levels and be able to hold yourself to them. Standards are codes of behaviour that you can choose to live by because you know you will make your life contended. Because they are the things that you personally honour. The standards can be about your health, soul, relationship, approach to finances, and just about any area of life that you wish to improve. Quality consciousness is the belief that everything can and must be improved.

*"You can become an even more excellent person by constantly setting higher and higher standards for yourself and then by doing everything possible to live up to those standards".*

*— Brian Tracy*

In a world that is cutting corners, making compromises and thus competing on a downward path, let us compete on the upward path... let us not look at what to cut, but what to improve. Let us embrace quality and take quality to such standards that our competitors are left behind... let our own past standards be left behind... let us think and strive towards 'zero defect standards'.

> *"Be a yardstick of quality. Some people aren't used to an environment when excellence is expected".*
>
> — *Steve Jobs*

We ought to realise that Quality begins on the inside and then works its way out. The quality of what we give depends on the quality of what we have... the quality of what we have depends on the quality of what we do... and the quality of what we do depends on the quality of what we are. Quality is about not having a hole in your socks... no creaking doors... all the clocks in the house showing the same time... no torn upholstery... no leaking taps... the phone picked up within five rings... staff washrooms so clean that one can lie down on their floors...

Quality - the presence of which is seldom noticed, but the absence of which can never be missed. Quality is about detailed excellence in areas that no one might even notice... The most important thing about the beautiful lotus flower is that even after growing in murky water it is untouched by its impurity. Quality is the invisible detail... the presence of which makes all the difference. The roots of a lotus flower are in the mud, the stem grows up through the water, the heavily scented flower lies pristinely above the water basking in the sunlight. What makes the lotus flower so special? At night the flower closes and sinks underwater, at dawn it rises and opens again. Moreover, untouched by the impurity lotus symbolises the purity of heart and mind. This pattern of growth signifies the progress of self from the primeval mud of materialism, through the waters of experience, and into the bright sunshine of awakening. Thus, quality is the invisible detail... the presence of which makes all the difference.

## COMPONENTS OF QUALITY CONSCIOUSNESS

The three components of quality consciousness exist on an individual level. The first step is for the individual to develop awareness of his environment and the meaning of quality within it. The second step requires the individual to align her individual quality goals with those of the organisation for which he works. The final step for the individuals is to pay attention to what can be done to improve the present moment, blocking out distractions and negativity.

*"If it is the quality of your consciousness at this moment that determines the future, then what is it that determines the quality of your consciousness? Your degree of presence. So, the only place where true change can occur and where the past can be dissolved is the Now."*

*— Eckhart Tolle*

Let there be quality in everything you give, have, do, and... in what you are.

# Chapter 18
## RUN YOUR OWN RACE

# RUN YOUR OWN RACE

*"To run your own Race*
*do your own thing,*
*And live your own life*
*is the mark of true success"*

— *Robin Sharma*

Life is a multi-dimensional phenomenon. There are billions of people in this world. But everyone, each one of us, wants to become number one. Isn't it hilarious? Even if you become the country's prime minister or president, you would still feel that you are not number one. You may come across somebody with a very beautiful body — and rarely does one see prime ministers blessed with one! So far as beauty is concerned, even a prime minister may feel inferior to millions. And a president, he may feel inferior to those who are superior to him intellectually, who have created great works of literature and art. You may excel in some dimensions only, but you may desire to be excellent in all. Now, that is impossible. There are people who want to be number one even in being humble and modest! Imagine somebody being number one as being nobody.

Osho tells a Sufi parable: A great emperor; Nadir Shah, was praying. It was early morning; the sun had not risen and it was still dark. Nadir Shah was about to embark on the conquest of a new country, and was praying to God for his blessings, so he would be victorious. He was saying, "I am nobody. I am just a servant — a servant of your servants. Bless me. I am going on your behalf. This is your victory. But I am a nobody, remember." A priest was also by his side, functioning as a mediator between Nadir Shah and God.

Suddenly they heard another voice in the darkness. A beggar was also praying, and he was saying to God, "I am nobody, a servant of your servants." The king said, "Look at this beggar! He is a beggar and he says to God that he is nobody! Stop this nonsense! Who are you to say you are nobody? I am nobody and nobody else can claim this. I am the servant of God's servants. Who are you to say that you are the servant of his servants?" Now you see? It's all still there— the same competition, the same stupidity. Nothing has changed. The same calculation: "I have to be the last." The mind can go on playing such game with you if you are not intelligent. Osho suggests: Try never to be happy at the expense of another man's happiness. It's ugly and inhuman. Its violence in the true sense. If you think you can become a saint by condemning others as sinners, your saintliness is nothing but an ego trip. Truly we invite way too much grief when we play the foolish games of competition and comparison.

There is much despair in the world as everyone is trying to compete with everyone else. Only if we realised that we are unique, and must compete with ourselves alone. A wise aunt of mine once, advised me "My dear, never compare yourself with another. It makes you either vain or bitter." It was good advice but like most good advises, easier said than followed. We typically, compare our worst qualities with our perception of others 'best traits. Also, while comparisons require a metric, most things like beauty and goodness can't be measured. Comparisons are unfair. We get 86,400 seconds to seize the day and spending even a moment judging ourselves against others erodes our confidence and zest for life. Besides, there is no end to our desire to be better than others which often leads to discontentment and resentment towards others and ourselves. One has to drop this non-sense of competition.

## FINDING OUR NEW BEST

> *"Stop comparing yourself to others. You have your own race to run. Finish well"*
>
> — *Lecrae Moore*

Very often we come across stories of how we, the people, are full of stress and tension these days in order to reach the top of the ladder in thanks to rat race. We want the best of everything. But in the pursuit of 'the best' are we compromising with our happiness? Why don't we accept things? Why has it become so difficult for us to accept ourselves as we are; to be happy with our success and achievements; to truly value ourselves and our decisions regardless of what the world thinks or will think of us? In this world of mad competition and the unending rat race, everyone wants to be at top; everyone wants to achieve the best. It is perfectly fine to think out of box, beyond our comfort zone and to dream big. But at the same time, what is also important to know ourselves first. What we really want? And what have we achieved so far? Is the trade-off worth it? Everyone has a different potential, a different knack for things, a different capacity, a different background and a different story. Thus, for once, stop comparing our story with that of others and let us find our 'new' best… time and again.

## NO RUSH GO SLOW ATTITUDE

> *"Don't compare your progress with that of others*
> *We all need our own time to travel our own distance"*
>
> — *Jerry Corstens*

Even as people hare from one thing to the next in their pursuit of instant gratification, there are some who have made a conscious decision to go the wise tortoise way. Remember how your granny lovingly laboured over your favourite kheer, just that she'd get it right every time? Every ingredient that went to the kheer was specially sourced and from consistency of the milk to the degree of sweetness, the level of precision involved was time-consuming. In these days of instant kheer mixes, you would think poor granny's kheer-making ritual was a tad too tedious. That granny would disdainfully cock a snook at the just-pour-me-out mixes is a thought that may not occur to you. Why cooking, in these days of rap music and lyrics without break, pausing to catch your breath might also seem like a travesty. So, whether we are talking, walking, eating, praying or playing, it's almost as if we are on a perpetual fast forward mode. But wait a minute. It's not everyone who is doing the fast lane cruise. There is a growing breed of people that thinks life's futile if indeed there is no time to stop and stare.

Dr. C.L. Calridge now in her fifties, is a founding member of Footprint Choices, a group dedicated to furthering sustainable living— both environmentally and socially sustainable. As a supporter of the Slow Movement, she connects people throughout the world to enable them to reap the benefits of slow living. This no rush go slow attitude means working less. It means doing things with greater efficiency and yet taking on less stress. It means getting back to family values, meeting up with friends and not feeling guilty about enjoying leisure time.

We are so busy in the race of life, that we often forget to oil engines of the machine we need for everything that we do — our body. I just want you to take a moment and tell yourself that everyone is running their own race and that no one is running the same race. You can be your own winner, and so can everyone else in your life. Create an environment for yourself and everyone around you to grow, but not with your health at stake. It's time we pay more attention to our health instead of being engrossed in the rat race.

One has to be sensible. Understand your limitations and aspire not for what is impossible. Remember a rose is a rose. It cannot be a lotus, like a lotus cannot be a rose. Be yourself and just be! Don't strive to be number one. Run your own race and you will be in total bliss. The race is not always to finish. It is also a lot about how to get there. Joining the slow movement is not about renouncing the world or giving up earthly pleasures. It is about having the remote control in your hand and every so often putting the tabs on the speed limit.

# Chapter 19
# STAND UP FOR YOURSELF

# STAND UP FOR YOURSELF

*"Don't expect to make a difference unless you speak up for yourself"*

— Laurie Halse Anderson

Developing a healthy assertive attitude can transform every aspect of our lives; our work, our relationships, our appearance, the way we shop, the way we feed and clothe ourselves, the way we organise our finances, the way we spend our leisure time. Indeed taking time out for leisure in the first place is an assertive act. Being able to express feelings constructively and be open with others and ourselves about our needs, maximises our chances of getting what we want in all these areas. This in turn increases our confidence and our self-esteem, which enable us to become more assertive and so on. Real assertiveness does not happen overnight. Assertiveness is the ability to express yourself and your rights without violating the rights of others. It is approximately direct, open and honest communication which is expressive and self-enhancing. Assertiveness does not come from a textbook, self-help book or seminar; real self-assertiveness is born within. Many never understand the meaning of assertiveness in the first place: they believed, and still do, that it is just a slick cover-up for aggression. Some think that assertiveness is just a milder, 'nicer ' form of aggressiveness. Learning how to be assertive helps one protect one's boundaries, communicate effectively, save time for meaningful pursuits and builds self-love. It is the most potent way to remain assertive in all areas of your life. Love yourself to the point where you are able to reject anything or anyone unworthy of your time, energy and attention.

## BECOMING AN ASSERTIVE PERSON

*"One's philosophy is not best expressed in words, it is expressed in the choices one makes... In the long run, we shape our lives and we shape ourselves. The process never ends until we die. And the choices we make are ultimately our responsibility."*

— Eleanor Roosevelt

## IMAGINE THE FOLLOWING SCENARIO

You are standing in a line, say at a bank counter or a coffee shop, waiting for your turn to be served. Suddenly, someone cuts through and stands ahead, looking as if they have every right to be there, without so much as giving a glance backwards. No one seems to have noticed, or even if they have, no one is saying anything.

## WHAT DO YOU DO?

- Do you see the inside, unable to voice the words that seem stuck in your throat, your fists clenched in a tight fist, your nails digging into your palm?
- Or do you inwardly sigh, tell yourself that this is life, and this is how things are, and resign yourself to a little more wait time?
- Or do you tell the person to move away and go and stand at the back of the line. Don't they notice the line? You go on about the quality of their eyesight, their manners, their intelligence levels. You succeed in agitating yourself, and this heightened, hyper stimulation of your brain and heart takes a while to settle, perhaps taking a good part of your day.

- Or do you draw the attention of the person who has broken the queue to the fact that there is a line of which they were, perhaps unaware and suggest that they should take their place in it, as you and all others have been waiting their turn?

## LEARNING TO BE ASSERTIVE COVERS THE ENTIRE GAMUT OF:

1. How to stand up for yourself and not allow people to walk over you?
   
   On any given day, we face several situations where we need to assert ourselves. From someone cutting in front of you at Cafe Coffee Day, to your boss reprimanding you for being late( when you weren't), to a co-worker stealing your idea in a meeting, to your husband blaming you for something that wasn't your fault, to your child making you responsible for doing something for him...... the list is really endless. And yet, how often do you stick up for yourself or assert yourself clearly and firmly, without resorting to aggression or meekly giving away?
   
   It sometimes takes a crisis to precipitate angst or a realisation that our old methods don't seem to work anymore. We feel constantly drained, emotionally and physically, often overwhelmed and unable to cope with others and ourselves. We flare up at the slightest irritation, our nerves on edge, as we struggle with all that we have bottled up. We need to deep, discover from where this turmoil stems, and change some patterns of our reactions to effect new paradigms of behaviour, habits and attitudes.

We recognise that we need to standup for ourselves— the self is the core of who we are.

2. How to state your position or point of view firmly yet non-aggressively?

> *"Half of the troubles of this life can be traced to saying "yes" too quickly and not saying 'no' soon enough."*
>
> — Josh Billings

"I used to be a people pleaser. I tended to agree with whatever someone said, for fear that they would like me if I disagreed. I wanted to belong. After marriage, I wanted to fit in with new family, wanted them to like me, and I would go out of my way to help, even if I was tired. I realised, after a decade, that this is how they saw me accommodating, passive, always to be counted upon".

"After a while, I realized, I was burnt out and stuck in a pattern of interaction that I just could n't get out of, I told myself that next time, I will put my foot down, but I kept getting sucked into my self-made role".

What does it mean to be an easy walk-over? Why do other people find it easy to walk over you, and not say, your friend who always seems so sorted?

If you stay quiet for fear of not being liked, loved, wanted, appreciated, or validated or do something out of your way, at the cost of your time, effort, and willingness because you do not want to be considered selfish or unkind, and fear being rejected, ignored, or overlooked by loved ones, then this thinking will make you the perfect candidate for being walked over. Thus, the first step is to be aware of your intentions and your reason for not asserting yourself. " It is not selfish to love yourself, take care of yourself, and to make your happiness a priority".

Like everything else being assertive is a practice, and the more you practice the better you get it. For instance, be aware of your body language. Your posture, very often conveys whether you are a walk- over or can take a stand, and many of us are not cued in to how our body looks to others. You can practice this every day in order to ingrain it into your body.

- Stand up straight, breathe deeply.
- Make eye contact with people you are speaking to, get center over your feet, rest your hands at your sides, or gesture to make a point.
- Let your body communicate your confidence in who you are and what you have to say.

3. How to say "No"?

*"It's only by saying 'no' that you can concentrate on the things that are really important ".*

—Steve Jobs

One of the hardest parts of being assertive is learning the art of saying 'no'. Somehow many of us believe that it is not okay to say no. We wonder what the other will think...... we wonder if they will get hurt. Being able to say no is, one of the best signs of being in a relationship. We need to say 'no' when we don't want to be. Be it 'for' a relationship; or 'in' a relationship; be it for something as small as a dinner, or someone asks for your hand in marriage, the tiny decisions and the bigger ones - NO is okay. If you don't feel right, you have to say it. ASSERTIVENESS means not giving into situations that are not in your best interest.

4. Four ways to say "NO":
- One of the toughest hurdles to overcome is to decide whether the other person's request of you is reasonable. Don't look to decide whether the other person's request of you is reasonable; the simple fact that the request was made means that the person has decided that he/ she wants you to comply, regardless. Look inside of yourself first: If you hesitate or hedge or if you feel cornered or trapped, or you notice a tightness or nervousness in your body, it may mean that the request is unreasonable. Sometimes you may be genuinely confused or unsure because you just do not have enough information to know for sure.
- Example: 'NO' for an extra helping of food on your plate at a dinner party if you don't want it. 'No' for doing extra hours at the office when you'd rather not. Turning down projects or nights out with friends might not look like able, but occasionally saying 'no' allows you to say 'yes' to events and tasks that allow you to flourish. For the most part, you have the right to use your time as you fit.
- 'Being nice is really overrated'We keep postponing our stand till the other person starts taking liberties with us. It is better to assert yourself at the start of an interaction. In the first instance that someone crosses your boundaries or tries to make you do something that goes against what you want, you need to state in clear terms that it is not acceptable to you. Later after you have allowed someone to take you for granted or override your wishes, it becomes difficult to assert yourself.
- Third, practice saying, "no". It might be difficult at first but, with practice, you will see that exercising this right helps

you get ahead. Saying 'no' comes with a caveat, though. It should come out sounding firm, yet polite. Also, it should be said without sounding apologetic or making excuses, justifications and rationalisations.
- To consistently say 'no' with grace and clarity, we need a variety of responses. To some people, this comes naturally. Others however, offer noncommittal answers like 'I'll try to fit that in', or 'I might be able to' when they know full well that they can't. It's far better however, to offer a clear no than string someone along or give them a wispy- washy 'no'. Own your choice to say 'no', and it will come out naturally and effectively. Finally learn to say no without saying "I'm sorry" weakens your stand.

5. How to set boundaries?

A critical part of being assertive is to set boundaries. Boundaries determine what you will and will not tolerate from another person. It defines the point where you begin and the other person ends. It's a non-negotiable zone and you need to set it and value it and imprint it into every word and action. 'Healthy boundaries give you a sense of self. If you have weak boundaries, you may be easily suggestible. You may not be able to separate your emotions from that of others and may feel guilty for someone else's negative feelings or problems or accept blame easily. Clear internal boundaries help you know where your responsibilities end and those of others begin. You may tend to take on other people's feelings, thoughts, or beliefs as your own and lose your sense of individuality. This is called 'enmeshment'. It can be draining and emotionally exhausting.

Example: "Setting boundaries was not something I understood till very late in my life when I started getting ill and feeling exhausted." I learnt how to set boundaries very gradually. I learnt not to fix other people's problems, not to be available, and never to help unless asked or if I genuinely wanted to. I say I am busy if I don't want to see someone. The most important part is I don't feel guilty anymore. More people want to offload, want a willing ear. I do not listen, but when I start feeling drained. I make an excuse and come out of the situation.

6. Difference between setting boundaries and being aggressive:

- There is a marked line between setting a healthy boundary and coming on strong. A healthy boundary is not a reaction. It is having a civil conversation. It is agreeing to disagree and not walking away in a huff. It is choosing your battles wisely and not setting off on a warpath at every instance. It is being expressive not explosive.

- We can set boundaries by conveying what is acceptable to us. " You cannot talk to me like that". Being an example.

- Boundaries are easier to set when we are easier to set when we are self-aware and take time to introspect and observe ourselves, "We need to be brutally honest with ourselves first not necessarily with others."

- Healthy boundaries help set the tone for how you want to be treated in a relationship. They help you stay on in relationships that foster and enhance personal growth, make decisions that lead to self-

development and thus enhance your sense of well-being. Healthy boundaries help you balance self-interest and attainment of your goals, with that of helping others achieve their goals and interests.
- When we tell a child to keep quiet or not cry, we are not allowing them to acknowledge their emotions out without listening to them or giving them space to simply feel their feelings. We divert their minds, distract their attention, and this in turn, becomes a habit, ingrained into their system as they grow up. 'As adults, this starts a unhealthy pattern of distracting our mind with things like shopping, TV, food and alcohol, when we start experiencing strong feelings'. A child who is not able to process his feelings will not be able to stand up for himself to achieve and often training on other people in order to do so - or who is unable to say 'no' and takes on more than he is capable of.

7. How to communicate firmly, but in an unaggressive way?
*"Assertiveness is not what you do, it's who you are"*
— Shakti Gawain

"When things get heated up, I exit the situation after excusing myself, promising to continue the discussion after the other person has cooled down, so that we can converse without getting our emotions in the way." Having learnt this process after months of trial and error, I am now happy with the way I deal with conflict and dissent. Earlier, I would fly off the handle, storm out, burst into tears, or keep things simmering on the back burner of my mind for days on end. This keeps a potentially volatile situation from spirally out of context and control, and we leave the situation with respect and focus. Most importantly, we feel empowered.

8. Tips on effective assertive communication:
   - Asserting yourself should not come at the cost of another's respect. When you really assert yourself, it is done with the intention of conveying your needs and not with the covert aim of putting down someone else or getting back at them. Nor is it about breaching another's space but being at ease with your own and communicating that.
   - When you are truly assertive, you respect yourself as well as another. You take care to state your point in a calm, centered, and non- combative manner.
   - Assertive people recommunicate. Approximately in a direct, open and honest way, are respectful of personal boundaries, both theirs and other people's, say 'yes' when they want to and 'no' when they mean no.
   - Assertive people are able to give and receive positive and negative feedback and are able to handle conflicts and disagreements effectively.
   - It's important to tone the emotions down. Say what you need to with thought, not impulse. And take responsibility for what you say; do not blame others for your words or actions. You have to voice yourself.

9. Empowering Yourself to be Assertive - Tips and tools to develop your assertive muscle:
   Your mind is one of the most powerful forces on earth. It can be your strongest ally or your worst enemy. Here is a set of tools to enhance the part your mind plays in becoming assertive.

- Use 'I': If you want to show assertive behaviours avoid using 'you', because this stops you from allowing control of the listener. When you use me; you communicate your feelings and avoid the defensive attitude of your partner..
- Imaging: This process couples visualisation - creating images in your mind as if what you imagine is already happening - with the emotional desire to make it happen. If your image has been chosen from inner wisdom while you're in a relaxed frame of mind, it can become real in your life quickly and solidly. To become an assertive, create a vivid picture in your mind of how you would look, think and feel as an assertive person. Create the assertive you that you want. Concentrate on this message in moments of relaxation. The more detailed your goal, the better and faster it can be achieved.
- Watch your body language: The way you project, your body communicates if you can stand up for yourself or are submissive Keep your back upright and your shoulders pushed back naturally. You should not be tense but should be mindful of your posture.
- Be aware of your voice: The tone should be firm and even. Not too soft nor too loud.
- Maintain eye contact. Looking steadily into the other person's eye when speaking will convey that you are not intimidated or going to be manipulated.
- Avoid ambiguity: Be clear when communicating—stick to your point and be precise.

- Don't use rude language: Don't swear or talk rudely. Using obscenities does not show assertiveness. Instead it shows crude behaviour and immaturity of understanding. It demonstrates you cannot be taken seriously. Don't make personal references such as 'I don't like her', and do not get personal by name calling or sharing.
- Take a stand: Take responsibility for the point you want to make or the action you want to take. Don't apologise if you don't need it. Back up your points with facts.
- Grow with experience: Test yourself. Don't stick to your comfort zone; face people or situations where you don't feel the most comfortable. It will help you develop. Observe others and learn!
- Music: A powerful way to communicate with ourselves. Music reaches us at such a deep level at times it almost seems possible to feel it rearranging our molecules! It is definitely felt in the body as it is perceived in the mind. Movies use strong musical sound tracks to amplify the action.
- Treasure Maps: Perhaps the most playful tool is the treasure map. A visual tool that makes it easier for you to picture what you want; a treasure map is a more concrete way of telling your inner self what it needs to do to achieve your goals. A colourful drawing or collage that represents what you want can include all the things necessary to achieve your goal — much like scale drawings and models help architects and builders get the job done.

- Affirming: It can keep you from ruling your inner self causing you to act non- assertively or aggressively. Affirming is a way to be assertive with yourself. It is a creative, conscious process that enables you to express yourself more fully and confidently. An affirmation is a spoken and written declaration of something you want, phrased as if it were already happening. It is important to phrase your affirmation in a positive, proactive way. However, don't pressure yourself for instant results.

10. Affirmations for an assertive person:
    - I am becoming and assertive from inside out.
    - I am dissolving the barriers to my self- expression.
    - I feel more powerful.
    - I communicate more clearly and effectively.
    - I handle confirmation with greater ease.
    - I express my enthusiasm and joy more freely and fully.
    - I am becoming stronger and more courageous.
    - I am more and more pleased with whom I am
    - I am taking charge of my life.
    - I can create love, success and happiness for myself.

## CONCLUSION

When we respond out of choice, confidence, awareness, onus, and respect, which all arise out of knowing, listening, and working on our self at a deeper level and consistent practice, we truly assert ourselves. Asserting yourself is owing your space in this world with quiet grace, steady resolve, and innate strength. Who wouldn't want to be in such a space.

As Lao Tzu puts it so beautifully, *"Because one believes in oneself, one doesn't try to convince others. Because one accepts oneself, the whole world accepts him or her."*

# Chapter 20
## TAME YOUR TRIGGERS
## THE BEST VERSION OF YOURSELF

# TAME YOUR TRIGGERS

Many of us have a trigger for almost all our patterns whether it is healthy or unhealthy. It's so easy to fall into the rut of negative patterns. But can we replace these with healthy ones? Of course, we can! The trigger could be a location or time or emotion or other people or the last action.

*"Ideas pull the trigger but instinct loads the gun"*

— *Don Marquis*

For example, if I go out with that friend(other people), either I must smoke... If I go to cinema theatre (location), I must drink carbonated drinks... If I am angry or upset or depressed (emotions), I must fill with junk foods... Last time I saw tasty food (last action), I ate it and it was pleasurable; so, whether I am hungry or not, I should eat that food whenever I see it. Around 5 o' clock in the evening (time), I should have coffee... The list could go on and on.

Just take a moment! Spend a little time; analyse your experiences, analyse your subconscious patterns, try to find what your 'Trigger' is! Do not be a stranger unto yourself. Introspection will help you identify your 'Triggers'.

## WHAT IS YOUR TRIGGER?

When you react unusually to a situation, do you stop to wonder what is triggering that reaction? When you notice that your immediate reaction to a person or situation is overly emotional or irrational, it usually means that something has been building up or is hidden deep inside of you — such as anger, sadness, resentment, frustration, or a traumatic event and more. This reaction is known as an emotional trigger. We all have emotional triggers that are related to something specific. It could be a past event, a topic, a person, a place, a comment, a tone of voice etc. In most cases, the trigger is related to a past event, especially our childhood or during our adolescence. The trigger and the reaction associated with it is so quick, that we won't even recognise why this has happened in the first place.

In Catherine's (name changed) case, during her school days, her mother used to have an indifferent attitude whenever Catherine spoke about her day at school. As a child going through varied experiences in school. Her enthusiastic sharing about it was never listened to by her mother... (Who knows what inner battle her mother was fighting!)

Nevertheless, Catherine would always feel, 'No matter what elates me or upsets me, it's not a big deal'. So, for Catherine, her mother, being the person, she loved the most, wasn't emotionally available for her when she needed it. She used to express her anger by acting aggressively to get her mother's emotional attention. In her marriage life also, she suddenly gets furious on trivial matters. Once she was returning home after finishing a long day work, when her husband made a comment that she looked tired. She said, "Yes I had a bad day at work. Actually, I felt little upset because..." Before she could continue, her husband cut her off and said, "Oh that's not a big deal". He said this to lighten up the situation. Catherine suddenly got furious. She went to her room and banged the door close! After sometime, she started feeling bad for her earlier reaction towards her husband. The only question in her head was, "Why did I get angry? Why did I behave like this with my husband whom I consider the most loving person in my life?" After this episode she started watching TV keeping the volume very high, just to cope with her 'something' that had caused this behaviour. That something is nothing but a "Trigger".

What she believed was - when your emotions are not valued by your loved ones, the only way to get attention is through aggressive reactions. Perhaps a trigger is simply a stimulus that evokes upsetting feelings, which may lead to problematic behaviour all have triggers, and we all have unhealthy ways in which we deal them. For example, A person who felt ignored and dismissed growing up might start yelling whenever they feel they aren't being heard. A person who had emotionally unavailable parents (or partners) may get insecure whenever someone isn't there for them. A person who felt controlled in the past might get angry when they think they're being told what to do. A person who felt helpless for years might panic when they're in a situation over which they have no control. Some other coping mechanisms include running away from the spot, a complete shutdown for some time, blaming everyone or someone, getting addicted to food, shopping indiscriminately etc.

## FEW STEPS TO DEAL WITH TRIGGERS

*"We are not a victim of our emotions or, thoughts. We can understand our*

*triggers and use them as tools to help us respond more objectively"*

— *Elizabeth Thorton*

Do any of the above emotional triggers resonate with you? Ask yourself, "How do I handle it when it occurs?"

Step 1: Accept responsibility for your reactions: When you accept that only you are responsible for your triggers, you initiate the process of seeking the reason behind it.

Step 2: Identify the trigger: Most of us have no idea what our triggers are, so we first have to figure them out. We can do this by examining what makes us react so instinctively that we aren't to take a moment and pause because the pain or hurt is so intense.

Step 3: Stop blaming the poker: Our tendency is to validate the trigger by blaming the poker, getting people to agree with us and making a case in our head for why anyone would be upset by the poke. But it isn't people who trigger us. It's the fact that we have triggers.

Step 4: Respect your uniqueness and own it: This is your own unique trigger, so own it. Don't be afraid of it. Having triggers is human and everyone has them. You don't have to put them on parade, but you can talk about them privately to work through them.

Step 5: Actively shift your emotional state: You can practice this step at any time, even when you first notice a reaction to help you think through your triggers and responses. When you determine what you want to do next, shift into the emotion that will help you get the best results

Step 6: Relax: Breathe and release the tension in your body.

Step 7: Detach: Clear your mind of all thoughts

Step 8: Centre: Drop your awareness to the centre of your body just below the naval.

Step 9: Focus: Choose one key word that represents how you want to feel in this moment such as calm, patient, confident, courageous, or caring. Breathe in the word and allow yourself to feel the shift. Stop trying to managing your emotions. Instead choose to feel something different when an emotion arises. This is how you gain emotional freedom.

Once you identify the root cause, you are almost done! Remember! Awareness is the best tool for self-discovery. Self-awareness is being aware of your thought processes: your thoughts, how they affect your emotions and how emotions cause to act. It is stepping out of yourself to examine yourself. Self-awareness is the key to emotional intelligence. What makes you mad might not stop making you mad, but you will know how to respond effectively or how to not respond at all. People with high emotional intelligence step out of their emotions to process them effectively. This includes moving away or avoiding situations that you know will trigger certain undesirable feelings and reasons within you. If you cannot move away or avoid the situation, self-awareness enables you to redirect the energy you are putting in those emotions. Discover your triggers and deal with them!

# THE BEST VERSION OF ME

## TOTALLY OPTIMISTIC DAY (TODAY):

If you want to reach a certain destination, you will have to travel that far. If you want to cook a dish, you will have to gather all the ingredients add work on it. If you want to develop a habit, you will have to start acting on it. For any specific result that we need, 'ACTION' is a must. Just thinking about an outcome without working on it is like day dreaming. No one has ever achieved anything without taking an action. Beneath this action lies a motivator who lets us take those actions.

It is the 'PRESENT MOMENT 'or 'TODAY 'that gives an opportunity to take actions. We cannot do anything about what has already happened yesterday, and we cannot be sure about what will happen tomorrow. The only responsibility we can take is 'TODAY'. Today teaches us to take responsibility whereas lingering on the past and the future makes us develop an attitude of blaming. What we are seeking is not the old man in a new costume. We are seeking the new man... a new consciousnesses. Let the future be born from the future. Take a fresh canvas and paint a new creation. Let the next stroke be a fresh stroke and a corrective stroke. We cannot go back and make a brand-new start. But we can start now and create a brand-new end. Truly that's all it takes... to draw a line to your past and make a fresh beginning, the present moment. It is only moment that exists. It is indeed true. The learning that we have gathered from our past and the dreams that we plan to materialise in the future needs to be acted upon in the present moment.

While gazing out of the window, I saw a man sweeping old and dried leaves off the garden with a long broom. It instantly brought me to realisation that today is the time to clean and rectify all things happened yesterday. Today gives us an opportunity to believe in ourselves, then in our dreams. They are powered by a realisation of the constant love of Creator towards us as a lover. Today gives us an opportunity to learn from our mistakes, to correct them and not to repeat them. Today is the time when you can heal yourself, forgive others and to let go of all those things that we have held on to.

TODAY is a great 'Rectifier', 'Lover 'and 'Healer'. So today is the day when you can sow the seeds to plant a beautiful tree in the future. It is also the day where you will get the fruits of the seeds that you planted in the past. Thus, it gives you an opportunity to experience the fruits of your past actions. Today, from where I stand, it is fantastic to see where I started out. The turns that I took, the stopovers that I made, the speed breakers that I challenged, seem to have happened over many breaths. We do make a deal of all of this, but having said that, it is a big deal because I'm, after all, the universe to myself. My part in this game is important. The time that I have been given to walk on this planet affects the entire working of the universe. Make sure to use your today wisely, because soon your today will become 'yesterday'. Be the BEST VERSION OF YOU and today is the only moment that exists. Live in the present moment.

## EVERYDAY IS AN EXPERIENCE AND EVERY EXPERIENCE IS A LEARNING:

The beauty of life is in its unpredictability. Hence, it is better to make the best use of what we have at a given point of time, though something else always looks better. To a mind that is open to this truth every day is an experience and every experience a learning.

The job market was not at its best around the time Anu was completing her post-graduation in 'Human Resources'. There were hardly any companies visiting us for campus hiring. One of the few organisations that visited was a manufacturing company. As it was not an established brand, many of her classmates did not show interest. But she decided to appear for the selection process. At the end of the process, it was announced that she along with few other classmates, have been shortlisted for the final round that was scheduled a month or two later, after their final year semester exams. As it happened, she fell sick a day before the exams and was hospitalised for couple of days. Due to this, she had to miss most of her exams. This meant, she will be completing her PG program in only six months later. At a time when job opportunities were less, compounded her possibility of finding a decent job. Once all their exams got over, as scheduled, she along with other shortlisted classmates appeared for the final round of interview in the premises of the factory. Given that she was still recouping from her sickness and convinced that she will anyway be rejected, she appeared for the interview unperturbed and was quite confident about the outcome. However, she decided to give her best in the interview.

The panel was headed by a General Manager, Mr. Kiran Dani who headed that factory site. After a volley of questions from the panel came the final one from him, "Do you have any questions to us?" She replied, "I do not have any questions but I want to tell you that I fell sick and was hospitalised and hence could not appear for exams. Hence, I will not be completing my PG now. I am not sure if my college communicated this to you" I appreciate your honesty. Those exams do not mean much to her. However, you should complete your PG Program. Tell me, supposing we select you what support will you require for our end to complete your course? I could not believe what I heard but gave some suitable response to his reply. I still did not hope to get the job. But it so turned out that in her batch, she was the first person to get a job and joined it much ahead of others. When she looks back, if she had not taken part in that selection process it would have been difficult to land up in a job. In fact, at least couple of my batchmates, much more talented than her, never got into a HR career at all.

This gesture of the General Manager taught me an important lesson very early in my career that," To just follow the rule books, a leader is not required. Leadership is all about demonstrating empathy and taking exceptions under extraordinary circumstances." If you can use what is happening to you from outside, then you will realise that the journey empowers you; there is a lesson for the person in everything that happens. But the most fundamental is always 'GIVE YOUR BEST.' For in the end, BE THE BEST VERSION OF YOU, that is all that matters.

## CAN YOU SPREAD JOY IF YOU ARE UNHAPPY?

Even as a child I was a wonderer... I used to keep asking what is the purpose of love is. My fascination for love grew along with me. It introduced me to ups and downs and crazy topsy-turvy rides all of which seemed to keep revealing aspects of me to me. I realised I could love like anything when I found a relationship that allowed me to love like crazy. I realised, in adolescence that I could be a possessive lover when I was shown a fickle friend. I realised I could be unconditional in love when I saw love pours towards me. I could hate in love, and I could love in love. What I received I gave - during that phase. And love kept growing me, I outgrew the need to possess, I outgrew the need to own. I outgrew the need to give what I was getting. In the later stage I could see all the strongest of emotions in my family arise because of love - my husband Arun, my two sons as they were the ones, I had immediate access to. Being a very expressive person, extremely demonstrative of my love, this world of mine, had experienced all sorts of craziness from me. My focus turned towards creating an environment where my fragrance of love lingers... Anyone who comes into that space must feel at least a few drops of love showered on them. We were just flowing throughout the life doing seemingly ordinary things, the normal routines of the family, the giggles, the laughter, the surprise parties, games, adventures, thoughtful expressions, quality time, great food, memorable moments of togetherness, naughty pranks, cuddles, endless hours of chatting, being a pillar of strength and courage.... and the list just goes on. So, I asked myself the standard question - "What else can I do" Was this the purpose of love - to give and to take - I wondered? What more? How do I drench and soak these people in love? But this time, I didn't feel like doing anything. Expressing love was moving from the plane of doing to being there for them.

The love for what I do....
The love for what is...
The love for my past, my present, my future....
The love for life itself...

To drench all in love, the only choice was to make them experience the best version of me. I just wanted to soak myself into them, be with them and be there for them - no frills attached.

In order to help you relate better to what I am saying, let me give you the analogy of a rose garden. When we enter the rose garden, we can perceive the roses, the thorns, the softness, the petal formations, the soil and many other things. Yet the fragrance that we experience is invisible. We all know that fragrance is one such thing that makes us go back to the rose garden repeatedly. So, it was not doing something for my family anymore, it was about transferring my fragrance of love - the abundant, overflowing love I feel for my family onto them through subtle reassuring ways.

Some of them in my world were drenched in happiness and love. Some remained unhappy by choice. Someone sent me a beautiful message saying - thoughts of you are the background to my entire day. I am beginning to feel that way about love. You know how you go to a fine dining restaurant and there is a very elegant, beautiful piece of instrumental music either playing live or on a system? That's what love has become in life. A background music score which just soothes and makes sense in everything happening in the foreground. I no longer wonder about love.

Through this experience, I gained a series of realisations...

I realised how much I underestimated the seemingly ordinary days of my life. There is so much depth I could add by just soaking myself completely into that action.

I realised that happiest of all days was because of love, and the saddest of all days too was because of love. There was fear because of love and there was peace because of love. Love itself is a gift each one of us must gift ourselves. I can give to the world what I have. Anything and everything will trigger and cause a flowering of what's inside. So instead of trying to make my world happy, peaceful and loving, I am working on myself to be a happier, more loving and more peaceful person. By being the best version of me, anyone who comes near me receives joy, happiness and peace.

And the most profound of all realisations was - "I was given only to give." These days, it is becoming difficult to live even a moment without love. Whether I am eating or drinking, laughing or crying or screeching - there seems to be enveloping love all around. It was an experience that no amount of words can do justice to. With the mode of constant upgrading on myself to become the BEST VERSION of ME is the greatest gift, I can gift myself and my loved ones around me.

**BECOMING A BETTER VERSION OF YOURSELF:**

- **Mode of Constant Upgrading**

    I am really amazed to see how fast and frequently mobile phone companies release better version of their previous models. A lot of these are very small, incremental upgrades yet they release them to consumers who eagerly buy the upgraded versions. Whether it's technology or services, we want everything to be better than the old one. A few years ago, none of us would have thought that we would be able to book a cab by mobile. Paying for goods using a smart phone was a dream. Everything has changed, and we are constantly getting versions of the previous item. If you are not satisfied with the current version of yourself, then the quickest way to solve the problem is to begin working towards the better version of today. There is no 'right time 'to get started. With the Mode of Constant Upgrading on oneself to become the best version of yours is the greatest gift. You know, the one where you are:

- **More successful**

- **Doing what you love**

- **Existing as an overall happier person.**

Why not engineer a new life for yourself? Life is best described in the Present Continuous Tense-loving, learning, inspiring, growing, arriving, seeking, realising, becoming... in almost all aspects, professional and personal, expect more from yourself than you expect from the world. Also ensure, the standards you set for yourself is higher than the standards the world expects of you. Creating a better version of one's self simply means to take what already exists and improve upon it by adding, replacing or completely letting go of certain aspects of one's life. Equipping ourselves with new skills and getting over habits which we always wanted to eliminate can help a great deal in creating a 'better me. 'Fight your way to top. Go the extra-mile. Consistently surpass your own standards. Check the process and keep coming back till you win. Don't settle for anything less. Didn't W. Somerset Maugham remind us: *"It is funny thing about life; if you refuse to accept anything but the best, you very often get it."*

Life really begins to shift when we decide to become better than what we are. Most people feel dissatisfied with their lives because their life has become stagnant. They are not open to change or to learning something new. This idea of a 'better me' will help to push yourself to achieve your potential and open the doors to immense progress. For this to happen, we have to improve our physical self, our social self and our spiritual self. And nothing will improve by itself; we need to do things differently to make that happen. Take baby steps. It is wisely said, "A walking ant is better than a sleeping elephant." Stop looking for a secret trick. There is no miraculous short cut to the better version of yourself. You need to start from the beginning and take several small steps to achieve your goal.

Recognise that the best version of yourself should be your vision not anybody else's. Nothing falls into our laps; we need to plan and work hard. Your vision can be reached by tact, hard and smart work, the right timing governance and perseverance; and remember it happens admits tons of competition. Don't waste energy trying to live up to what somebody else want to be. In other words when you contemplate your better version, don't change yourself from who you are. Getting inspired by somebody is different from comparing yourself with someone. People depict an extremely exaggerated version of their life on social media platforms like Facebook, Instagram, Snapchat, etc. We only share the good things, not the bad. So, when you compare yourself to what you see on social media, you're only hurting yourself. We are one and only legitimate frame of reference. So, it will help if we track ourselves against our own self of yesterday. Here a little self-love can go a long way when it comes to liberating ourselves from the shackles that comparison wraps around our psyche. When comparing ourselves to other, we sometimes feel like we've missed the boat'. It's a thought that breeds resignation and fuels self-pity. In reality there is no other boat! We are the only boat in our life.

Another great way to upgrade yourself is to feed the mind constantly learning and growing. Knowledge is a bottomless pit, so keep learning something new. Listen to podcasts, read books, purchase audio books, join a book club, utilise search engines, watch documentaries or educational videos, subscribe to feeds of interesting information or play online games or programs that challenge your knowledge. Stretch yourself. Remember this saying: "Behind every unrealised personal growth goal, lies an overworked snooze button."

Do what you think best for you. Understand yourself, constantly evaluate yourself and estimate your potentials; work hard towards making your dreams a reality. You may get branded as a rebel, but think about the big picture. How does it matter if you're a rebel when you're doing what you want to, when you want to, unless it is hindering others around you? Playing safe doesn't make you smart, it merely makes another victim to the relentless deceit of societal pressures. When you do what you like, you obviously put your heart and soul into it, which only garner positive vibes for you and for the people around you. Constantly move beyond your comfort zone. Making yourself a little uncomfortable allows you to grow because you experience something new. When you are learning something new, you'll bump into the walls of your comfort zone, but you will climb over them.

Keeping up with your better self is not an easy task. Our time is limited. Choose what is most important right now and gently release yourself from the not so important things. This will help in striking that powerful balance that we strive for— the balance between happiness in the moment and action towards the better version of ourselves. This better version of yourself is slightly ahead of where you are now. The version who is a little more evolved gets up a little earlier and is a little better at focusing on the task at hand. It's the person you know you could be if you just try a little harder. It's not impossible, but you will need to push yourself harder to get there.

Let's move through life at 100 mph, striving for the next milestone and reaching for the next moment of grandeur. Becoming the best version of yourself is a marathon, not a race. If you run, you'll be grasping for breath pretty soon. Regularly hit the refresh button on your definition of your best self. Ralph Waldo Emerson says, *"Make the most of yourself.....for that is all there is of you."* Our life is our signature creation; let's aspire to become the best version of ourselves.

## SWEET ARE THE USES OF ADVERSITY

Each moment of life is an opportunity for self-growth. And opportunity mostly comes disguised as adversity. I remembered the meaning of the phrase, "Sweet are the uses of adversity!" All of us have to take the ups and downs of life. Just when you feel that you have finally gotten over the worst life will belt out a super-duper knock that will send you cowering on your knees. Most of the time you have no choice. You have to take what comes to you. But how you face the problem depends entirely on your attitude. You can face it squarely, look at it firmly in the eye and do the best possible thing under this circumstance, or (dare I say it?) sit down and give in and weep a painful. Most often than not, I strike a compromise. First, I sit down and get it out of my system by talking to my loved ones. While the moment to seize a lucrative opportunity may not come every day, life without a doubt, is an opportunity to grow and evolve consistently. Only when you have done the required inner and outer work does the life - changing opportunity fall into your grasp. Viewed this way each moment of your life becomes a precious opportunity to review it, tweak and make amends, and become a 'BETTER VERSION OF YOURSELF. ' Not only that, opportunities make themselves available to us only when we are grateful for whatever we have in life. If we are arrogant, critical, entitled, and ungrateful, we will soon see the river of opportunity of life dry up before our eyes. Mostly, our eyes open at the far end of our lives when we realise that the lost time and opportunity cannot be regained.

"Amazing Arunima":

Arunima Sinha, sportsperson and mountaineer, has turned tragedy into opportunity. At 23 her leg was amputated and she was disabled for life. Just two years later, at 25, she had climbed Mt Everest with an artificial leg and an injured spine! Today, she is all the rage on social media and inspiring millions with her fantastic story. At 23, national volleyball player, Arunima Sinha, was thrown out a moving train by four men, who was trying to snatch her gold chain. She lay in pain the whole night on the railway track, screaming help and bleeding profusely. Rodents fed on her; 49 trains passed over her. The next morning, she was finally discovered and taken to hospital. Her leg was amputated. Her spine was fractured. She spent six months in hospital. She and her family also suffered the indignity of national newspaper describing this as a suicide attempt on her part! Fed up with people's pity - What will she do with her life now? She'll never get married- and the demeaning publicity. Arunima decided she must do something impossible to make people realise her true worth. She decided to climb Mt Everest! She did not go home after being released from hospital. With the support of her brother-in-law, she went straight to meet Bachendri Pal, the first Indian women to have scaled the Everest. With Bachendri's warm support and encouragement, she trained in mountaineering for two years. She also received a sponsorship of Rs 50 lakhs from the magnanimous corporate, Tata Steel, for her Everest journey.

At 10.55 am on May 21, 2013, Arunima Sinha achieved her goal. After an arduous 52-day climb, she unfurled her Indian flag at the top of Mt Everest. Her excitement knew no bounds. "I felt like throwing my arms in the air and screaming," she says about her moment on Mount Everest." I wanted to tell everyone that I'm on the top of the world especially to those people who thought woman and an amputee could't do it. I took off my mask and my Sherpa(guide) just stared at me". Now at the top of the world, Arunima sees her future life as a fresh opportunity to train handicapped children in sports. Her project needs 25 crores and she states she doesn't even have Rs 25,000. "But this doesn't deter me", says Arunima. I climbed the world's highest peak when I didn't have a leg. What, then, is 25 crores? Arunima is an inspiration on how to live with joy and courage. She changed the root word 'problems' to 'challenges' and suddenly it seems surmountable conquerable. It depends on whether we want to look at the overall beauty of the painting or focus on that one grey cloud in the blue sky that is in the painting.

Arunima faced adversity head-on, firmly believing she had nothing to lose. As a drowning man grasps at any straw, she grasped misfortune with both hands, turning it into a life changing opportunity. Arunima's example tells us that what takes us to the end of the world can bounce back us to the top of the world if we can face our fears with patience and perseverance. I think to reach anywhere in life no matter what you are doing, there is some amount of struggle involved. For me, I am not fond of writing about the struggle that I've been through, but I feel very humbled when I think about it. I think that the struggle is what keeps you grounded. It's more like the goal should be to BECOME THE BEST VERSION OF YOURSELF. Life is like a blank canvas on which you can paint and draw whatever you want. It's all about courage, conviction and being open minded about the purpose of life.

# Chapter 21
# UPGRADE YOURSELF

# UPGRADE YOURSELF

*"Upgrade yourself*
*Because if not*
*No one will do it for you".*

— Kristine Quinlat Rernolla

Upgrade yourself every moment. You live You learn. Then you upgrade. You have to keep evolving and recreating yourself. Read, explore and discover. Learning new things and expanding your mind will add versatility into your life. From career aspirations and basic everyday changes to big life changing dreams, write freely. This is a judgement-free zone. Organise your wishes. Categories them into subsections like health, finance, relationship etc. Underline the big shifts you expect to make. Get a bird's eye view of your priorities. Ask yourself what can be achieved now and what you can do in next few months, and in long term. You shouldn't be who you were last week. Create new habits and consistently upgrade yourself in all ways and in all levels.

## STAMP OF APPROVAL:

*"It's not the end yet*
*Upgrade yourself and*
*Be your best version"*

— *Lumin*

Are you addicted to approval and acceptance? Are you always fishing for compliments to feel good about yourself? Would you please others than please yourself. We are so emotionally dependent, that just anybody can ruin us. If we are invited to a party, we feel rejected or humiliated. If people don't compliment us on our dress, we feel neglected. If people don't like our pictures on Facebook, we feel anxious, offended, and in severe cases depressed. Incidentally, now we have begun to depend on virtual feedback to feel good about ourselves. We are constantly mulling over what people said, how they behaved, or what they think about us. Consider these internal monologues: "Please tell me my cocktail gown is gorgeous." "Why is nobody commenting on my look." "Please tell me one good thing about myself so that I can happily get through the rest of the day." "Why is no body telling me I have lost weight?" "Do they think I'm dim witted?" We are begging for attention, affection and approval because we are deficient within. We are desperately empty inside, so we depend on public approval to fill the void. People are afraid to tell us that they don't necessarily like our fashion sense or that we gained weight because it might offend us. So, some of them say the opposite of what they really think. We have forgotten to express ourselves truly and freely because we want to please each other all the all the time. Likewise, the slightest unpleasant remark causes us to overreact. It causes some degrees of anxiety, pain, and general disturbance. Our emotions are contingent on what other people think and say and how they behave. Such is the alarming level of inner sensitivity. We internalise so deeply that it begins to affect our physical health too. We allow every comment, every event, and every situation to leave impressions inside of us, and then we cling to those impressions inside of us, and then we cling to those impressions for the rest of our lives. You are more important than you think you are, you are braver, you are more lovable and smarter than you think you are. UPGRADE what you think!

## SIFTING THROUGH LIFE CHAOS:

*"The ability to Upgrade is important"*

— *Scott Briggs*

A life audit is an exercise in self-reflection that helps you to clear the cobwebs of noisy, external goals. It is the spring-cleaning for the soul. Life can be crazy and goes by so fast that we get busy in reacting to it rather than creating it. "A life upgrade is vital if you want to be in charge of life rather than let it take the charge of you." Normally people loss their track of priorities because they are constantly caught in a frenetic pace, work load, more family responsibilities and people's expectations. That's why it's important to introspect and make a personal audit. Ask yourself what makes you happy, what fulfils you.

## SET A GOAL:

*"Sometimes, life can get in the way of itself. Every now and then it's important to take a step back and check how we are doing".*

— *Ximena Vengoechea*

Revisit and upgrade your wheel of life every few months to make sure you are on track, or to change your preference. An audit, at least once in a year, also make us realise if our goals have changed as we have evolved. Ask yourself simple questions 'Am I doing what I want to with my life?', 'Am I fulfilled?' Then you will realise that half the things you were running after had lost meaning in your life. Reassessing goals helps you to realise whether you want to focus on old bucket list or do a holistic overhaul.

## START SMALL TO FINISH WELL:

*"Vision is the art of seeing what is invisible to others"*

— *Jonathan Swift*

Architecting life takes time; time that we don't have in a digital age. Focus on your future plan and take simple steps to small successes. In time, they will transform your life completely. Life is, by design, a constant process of reinvention to move out of our comfort zone. Thus, take up something that is relatively easy and achievable to begin with. Do not bite off more than you can chew at one time. It takes time to develop your will power. Start with something small and accomplish it before you move on to something else. Do one thing at a time and do it well. Build your successes, reward yourself in some way and you will progressively become stronger. Thus, you can equip to upgrade yourself to handle larger goals successfully.

Upgrading requires time, honesty and guts. And if we are able to bite the bullet, the results are magical and priceless. Not using it is tantamount to having a Mercedes purring in your garage and rattling around on a scooter. Upgrade yourself.

## Chapter 22
# VALUE YOURSELF
# VICTORY OVER YOURSELF

## VALUE YOURSELF

*"Self-worth comes from one thing— thinking that you are worthy"*

— *Wayne Dyer*

Your own value is determined not by what you are, but by what you are able to make of yourself. In our life, there are many obstacles that we come across and most importantly, many milestones we achieve which feed our confidence and self-respect. However when we are awarded with an achievement and people applaud us, in that crowd you are bound to find one person or may be more than one who will be waiting for a chance to point out some fault in your success and project it as a failure right in front of your eyes. Criticism is not necessarily negative. It can spur us to do better. For a canvas to become a work of art, it has to lose its identity and be exposed to vibrant colours. Criticism must shake you to your roots and must drop you down several times, and that should give you enough time to gather all your energy and rise up with a force surpassing all limits. How the world behaves is none of our business. The greatest pride is in rising in your own eyes. How much ever you are tested, wherever you go, whatever you do... live your character.

### ACCEPT YOURSELF TO BE ACCEPTED:

*"You can search throughout the entire universe for someone who is more deserving of your love and affection than you are yourself, and that person is not to be found anywhere. You, yourself, as much as anybody in the universe, deserve your love and affection".*

— *Buddha*

None of us like the thorns, however, that doesn't make a rose despicable. In fact, the rose acknowledge that the thorns are a part of it, accepts them and love them. Now the choice is left to us whether to hate the thorns or to love the petals. Love every folly, every weakness and every mistake because each of these is a very much a part of you. Do not dissect yourself into things you like about yourself with the dissected parts. All that is good about you and all that is not good about you together is what defines you. You are you. You need not be someone or something to be you. Not being what others are and what is being yourself and remember, being yourself is what it means to be unique. Observe or recapitulate your college or school days. There will be one in every batch or group of yours who is not good at anything but is always happy, great to be round and most importantly, valuing himself / herself as much as they do others. These are the people who love themselves, accept every bit of themselves and are connected with themselves. Don't put your endeavour to shape yourself into a better being. Go after yourself only when you feel there is something wrong about you and not when others care for something that's distinctively a segment of your character. Everything that is right about you needs to be loved by you. Accept that moment in you, accepting when you don't have to hide from yourself — love that someone in you, loving when you feel complete all alone. The more you value yourself the less nonsense you tolerate.

## NEVER LOSE YOURSELF:

*"Stop begging and fighting for people to love you the right way. Stop investing time in people who don't mind if you stay or leave."*

*— Reyna Biddy*

Oftentimes, our need to be in a relationship is so strong that we ignore the obvious red flags in it, only to be shattered later on. Whereas if we placed self-love, self-respect and dignity over anyone or anything else, we would be able to foresee if a person we want to be with is the right one for us or not and prevent a major disaster from happening. If your lover is disrespectful to you, doesn't care for your feelings, manipulates, controls, emotionally blackmails you, or forces you to be someone you are not, then it's time to stand up for yourself and choose yourself over the relationship. Never abandon yourself, your priorities, career, friends, and goals for someone who deprives you of these things in the name of love when you are happy inside out, only then you will be able to nurture your relationship with happiness. Try to be authentic as you can be. Be you - the world will adjust. Never lose yourself.

## SET HEALTHY BOUNDARIES:

*"Learn to value yourself, which means fight for your happiness".*

— *Ayn Rand*

The process might look complicated... but it is worth it! Yes, you may not be perfect, you may not be perfect daughter, you may not be perfect partner, you may not be perfect friend, you may not be the perfect example, but one thing I know for a fact is that you sure don't care about what people think of you. You are what you. You are not going to change because cultural manual says so. You are not going to change because of the way society looks at you. One thing that really bothers you is noisiness and uninvited interference by the society. In my society, everyone has a say in your personal life. This noisiness extends to bizarre ends. Taste in music, favourite sport, the food you eat, the stuff you drink, the clothes you wear, the car you drive, the school you study in, the person you are married to, the school your child's going to enrolled in, almost everything! Is there no concept of healthy boundaries? On the top of it, they think that they are being helpful. What should we do in such a situation? Do what you think best for you. Understand yourself, constantly evaluate yourself and estimate your potentials; work hard towards making your dreams a reality. You may get branded as a rebel but think about the bigger picture. How does it matter if you're a rebel when you're are doing what you want to unless, it is hindering others around you? Playing safe doesn't make you smart, it merely makes you another victim to the relentless deceit of societal pressures. Take some risks happily. When you do what you like, you obviously put your heart and soul into it, which only garner positive vibes for you and for the people around you.

## FOSTER HEALTHY RELATIONSHIPS:

*"The only people who appreciate a doormat are people with dirty shoes."*

— *Leo Buscaglia*

Why is adequate self-worth so crucial to one's behaviour? As the term suggests self-worth is an inner conviction that one is worthy, whole and deserving of love, having a sense that life is perfect rather than unjust and unfair A strong sense of self-worth can only come from within. You can gauge if you have sufficient self-worth by simply observing closest relationships. Are you able to accept those you live without being judgmental and critical of them? If you have good relationships — are at peace with those nearest and dearest to you, then this indicates a healthy self-worth. In such a case you are at peace with others and very importantly with yourself. You can live your life joyfully and creatively. By the same token a lack of self - worth has the opposite effect and deprives you a sense of peace. Since you feel a lack within, you try to fill from without. Your fear that you are unworthy, imperfect and inadequate. This sense of lack feeds the ego — the seat of fear and allows it to take control of your life. Your ego now perceives itself as lacking and therefore flawed. In to rectify the situation and counter the lack within it seeks as to find flaws in others and their behaviour. It prompts you to run others down and to highlight what you perceive as their faults and failings in an attempt to prove that you are better than them. Thus, you try to derive your feeling of worthiness externally, by convening yourself and then setting out to convince others — that you are right, better smarter, more sensible than those around you.

## TREAT ME RIGHT:

*"You as much as anyone else deserve your love and respect"*

*— Buddha*

Recognising the importance of setting boundaries, one of the most important things that we need to learn as adults is how to get treated right. To teach people how to see us. In the name of love, too many of us become door mats. In your journey of ensuring the people to treat you right, be it personally or professionally, following tools will help:

## BUILD YOUR SELF-RESPECT:

One of the biggest issues that the world faces today is of low self-esteem. We don't love and respect ourselves enough. To make up for this lack that we feel within, we keep expecting to love and respect us all time in a way we want. When this doesn't happen, the vicious cycle continues and we feel even more low about ourselves. Our self-esteem is our responsibility. By improving ourselves by regularly working on our body-mind-spirit, by ensuring that we did enough thing that helps us in our growth, we can start moving towards a healthier self-esteem. People who feel good about themselves - who are bustling with energy, love for life and who are aligned with the law of Universe - don't feel the need to treat anyone poorly. In fact, they love to boost others. In short, the greatest pride is none of our business. The greatest pride in rising in your own eyes. How the world behave is none of our business? How much ever you are tested, wherever you go, whatever you do... live your character. Let the limitations of other people not limit us. 'Someone is wrong' isn't an excuse for us to be wrong. Wrong as a response to wrong isn't the way. Let us not trade our goodness. At every opportunity, let us not go ahead of people and not even with them. Never become an unwanted intruder into your progress. Always, flow with the flow.

# VICTORY OVER YOURSELF

*"The first and the best victory is the victory over yourself"*

— *Plato*

Most of us are slaves to habit and familiarity. Our present environment is a symbol of our present thoughts. My family is me; my job is me; my friends are me. It has been observed a wounded animal will return to what is familiar. Because man is also an animal, he likes familiarity and in time of trouble will also return to what is familiar. It is no wonder old habits die hard. How do we break away from habit? What is the secret of changing a lifetime of habit? How does one go about changing years of habit? Meaningful change does not have to come by hitting yourself over the head with a hammer nor do you have to sign up for courses or college. Change can come fairly easily, in simple steps, which are subtle and for the most part unnoticeable. Your old habits, routines and ruts, the same food, the same conversations, the same work, laziness, indifference, reluctance are all aspects of your old self. The old self you who adheres to comfort and the mundane. Before change can come there needs to be a desire for change. A complete life style makeover can be accomplished over a period of time without the trauma from hitting yourself over the head with a hammer. Habits are physical demonstrations of a mind that is boxed. There is no growth in repeating steps. The very meaning of life is movement.

## CHANGE INVOLVES EFFORT:

Lasting change does not come with making a change, but with commitment to keep changing until it becomes a habit— a habit of change. Change involves effort, devotion, commitment and sacrifice. The older version of yourself manifests itself in the things you end, the people you spend time with, the way you work, the job you have it comes in the form of hobbies. where you spend your time, how you conduct yourself. One of the best times to start your change is first thing in the morning. Commit yourself to making at least one tiny change every day and it doesn't have to be the same change. Try turning your alarm ahead or back 10 minutes. In other words, get up at a different time tomorrow morning. Probably no one will ever notice. Or try leaving your house 15 minutes early for work one morning or take a different route— you will see new people and different things. If you truly want change, growth, achievement, passion, happiness, victory— then you will have to struggle with your old self daily. Beat him into submission, struggle the life out of him and leave him dead in your wake. True victory requires constant vigilance, to be on guard against the old routine. Avoiding the well-trod path of the way things used to be. A battle against comfort and convenience.

## BEGINNING OF A SMALL VICTORY:

*"Even a small victory over yourself makes you a lot stronger"*

— *Maxim Gorky*

Make small subtle changes which will not upset your life or those around you. Make this your priority everyday — to do something different. Yes, we should look and aim to scale stars, Edmund Hillary, who succeeded in summiting Mount Everest, was not successful in his first effort; he made several tries before he succeeded. He would say that even the highest peak has limits and cannot grow further and taller but that he could do and grow to improve his performance. Somebody said that we should compete with ourselves and improve our performance every time. In gymnastics, new records are constantly made, only to be broken after sometime. Thus, small victory is the beginning of a defeat which could be the beginning of a successful victory. View failures and defeats as only postponed success. Let us treat defeat as the fertilizer for victory.

## SELF-PITY IS AN OBSTACLE TO VICTORY:

*"If you believe in yourself and have dedication and pride and never quit, you will be a winner, the pride of victory is high but so are the rewards".*

— *Paul Bryant*

Self-pity is a real danger to your success. Don't dwell on negative things in your life unless you can change them. But if you can't, change your attitude by looking at them from different angles, and don't let them interfere with the things you can do something about. Since we can be our own worst enemies, your bigger victories in life will be those you win over yourself. Understand and know your strengths to then build upon them. Ascertain what is best for you and you go for it. The dedication and persistence you need to succeed can only come from within.

As you cultivate your habit of change, you will begin to make bigger changes and you will start ranging out. Your growth will start to accelerate and you may find yourself in conflict with those around you and who know you the best. So, to sum up: the greatest victory is victory over yourself. You can be different, you can be successful, you can be the change, because you are an uncommon breed and you are bound to live a great life, leaving an impressive legacy for future. It is all in your hands!

## Chapter 23
# WONDER YOURSELF

# WONDER YOURSELF

*"When I admire the wonders of a sunset or the beauty of the moons, my soul expands in the worship of creator."*

—*Mahatma Gandhi*

Our ability to wonder is the magic key that unlocks the scintillating world of discovery, invention, knowledge, play, and finally our inner self. Look at world around you, open your mind as well as your eyes, you would be surprised what you find. Wonder keeps you rooted in the present and is constructive. Sometimes, the small things in life can get you down. And, it is the small things in life that can uplift you as well. Like the beauty of a humming bird's nest. How courageously this bird holds up through wind, rain, thunder and lightning. How hard their lives are! But no matter what obstacles lie in their path, they master them, overcome them and survive. They keep flying, they keep singing and making nests. The more people wonder about the universe, the more they will have desire to understand it, and the less inclined they will be to destroy it. Thus, it's wonder that makes the present exciting and the future secure.

## WONDER IS FOR ALL:

> *"Open your eyes*
> *to the beauty around you*
> *Open your mind*
> *to the wonders of life*
> *Open your heart*
> *to those who love you*
> *and always*
> *be true to yourself"*
>
> — *Donna Davis*

Every generation has two sets of people — the movers and the shakers, and the rest. It's not necessary for everyone to be a mover and shaker, but it's imperative for everyone to be overwhelmed by Creation once in a while, to get a broader perspective and on everything and, thereby, become a little self-centred. We love the thrill the amusement park gives us. People volunteer for adventure rides and sports like falling off a cliff, parasailing, jumping off planes for sky diving. The rush of adrenaline excites us and gives us a sense of winning. "But you can't depend on adventure sports to get your daily dose of wonder, right?" The idea is not to depend on extreme physical stimuli to be struck with wonder. That would be ridiculous, not to mention fatal" Then what does an ordinary man need to do to reboot and refresh regularly?" Learn to look at everything differently. Look with the eyes of a child, as if you were looking it for the first time. Or look as if it were the last time. Wouldn't you look differently then? Try that, and you might even find the Divine behind the mundane, mystical, unpredictable, paradoxical life. We can also learn to live each moment completely by observing how a cyclone operates. The cyclone creates havoc all around, but the epicentre of the cyclone called 'The eye' is the calmest and quietest. Similarly, whatever life throws at us, if we can operate from our epicentre (our centeredness), then life will become one eternal wonderland — our personalised playground or amusement park.

## NATURE IS WONDERFUL:

*"To see a world in a grain of sand*

*And a heaven in a wild flower,*

*Hold Infinity in the palm of your hand*

*And eternity in an hour"*

— *William Blake*

The vastness of the oceans and seas, the altitude of the mountains and valleys, the variety of the trees, flora and fauna, the birds and the bees, the animals and many creatures, the sun, the stars and the moon - everything created is one big present, and I found myself unwrapping it all from the universe—I was surprised! I rejoiced, and I whispered thank you to God for creating a world so mighty and big, so beautiful and scenic! I am moved as I can feel the damp grass; feel the softness of the fur of a pet; experience tenderness in touching the petals of a flower; relish the juicy fibre and pulp of the fruits. I get surprisingly intoxicated as I've been stopping to breathe the fragrance from the earth; enjoy the aroma of the flowers, leaves and trees; the smell of the fresh air and the morning breeze; the scent of the sea from the shells and the fragrance of a new-baby. My eyes sparkle with admiration and I am discovering the glistening dew drops on the leaves; the soothing light of the twinkling stars, hundreds of kilometres away, and the gentleness of the moonlight which comforts the eyes; the brightness of the sun. I find wonderment in looking into my own eyes! As I walked a little ahead, a cool breeze gently kissed my face. It was refreshing and made me smile. I turned and could see no one around who was blowing air my way! "Where is this air coming from? "I asked myself. It's something that happens so often to many of us and seldom do we pause and recognise it or be wondered. The list is endless. I realise that there are infinite wonders created by the Almighty for all of us. We need to discover them and pause to appreciate and thank the creation for this Beautiful World. I am all set, finding my presents and unwrapping them, one at a time. I hope you too will set out and look out. Let's find our wonderland every day — one at a time.

## WONDER, A MYSTERIOUS SOURCE OF DISCOVERY:

*"The most beautiful thing we can experience is the mysterious; it is the source of all true art and science".*

*— Albert Einstein*

Newton wondered about a falling apple. Fleming about bacteria, and the world was never the same again! What if Archimedes hadn't had the Eureka moment? What if Copernicus hadn't wondered, or Columbus wandered? The world would be much poorer if Shakespeare hadn't exclaimed, *"O wonder! How many goodly creatures are there here! How beauteous mankind is!"* and let his imagination flow! It is wonder that transformed an illiterate simpleton into great 5th century writer and dramatist of Sanskrit literature, Kalidasa, who wonderstruck on beholding the beautiful form of Goddess Kali spontaneously broke out in praise of her in lyrical Sanskrit. Philosophers wondered about God and theologies were born. Sages wondered about the universe and the scriptures were born. Thus, for one who cares to pause and wonder, every being, every thought, every act and everything in the world is an object of mystery to unravel, a puzzle to crack. Any path breaking invention, discovery or creative expression could only be a result of wonderment. Artists and scientists, doctors, and industrialists, mystics and philosophers, kings and leaders all of them wondered and helped the world go round a little more merrily! But these were extraordinary visionaries, and We, an idle wonderer without enough steam to erupt in creativity. In fact, we too count in the cosmic scheme of things?

## WONDER CAUSES SELF-DISCOVERY:

*"Mystery creates wonder and wonder is the basis of man's desire to understand"*

— *Neil Armstrong*

The phenomenon is of absence, not presence, as Osho would put it. "Up there, amid the magnificence of the towering Himalayas, you, with your expectations and prejudices, desires and fears, attachments and repulsions, were absent. You, with your open mind and heart and entire being, were present. The past and future ceased to be; you were jerked into the present. In that eternal moment the mind was incapable of going on with its constant chatter of remembering, recording, analysing, judging, explaining and verbalising. Your usually fragmented senses integrated to create an intense awareness and experience."

In fact, such experiences can melt away the separation between you and the mountains. You feel as if you were an organic part of the whole scene, like a mountain lion — you totally belonged there. When one comes face to face with something that is unexpected, extraordinary and inexplicable, the mind stops, the identification with body mind complex ceases, and that's the reason you feel one with the Universe. "Existence reveals itself to one who wonders". And the magic never ceases even after you discover how it works. That is why an Einstein could still exult over a ray of light, because as he remarked, "we still do not know one thousandth of one percent of what nature has revealed to us.". And that is why one will never again take two plus two for granted, because it expresses a thought of God, as it did to 'The Man who knew Infinity '— Srinivasa Ramanujan.

Directed by whom does the mind go towards objects? Commanded by whom does the life force move? At whose will do men utter words? What power directs the eyes and ears? 'To wonder about the Himalayas is fine, but to ask 'who' wonders is the crux of it. Who is the one throwing light on the Himalayas so that it can be perceived? By whose grace do the eyes perceive its beauty? Who, who, who... Shine the torch of wonder inwards and ask the mother of all questions — Who Am I? When one persistently and unrelentingly engages in self— enquiry, the body mind complex will be dissolved forever, leaving behind the Universe itself, and an awareness of existence that is ever wonderful blissful... Wonder is the foundation of yoga, the divine harmony of creation. The entire cosmos was thus poised in constant wonderment!

# Chapter 24
# XESTURGY OF YOUR INNER SELF

# XESTURGY OF YOUR INNER SELF

Xesturgy is the process of polishing the inner self. What's inside only comes out. It's what is under the ground that creates what is above the ground. It is the invisible creates the visible. It is the inside that creates the outside.

A thought popped up into my mind. Isn't it a fact that everything which we look at in our life has another side which is unheard, unseen, or not thought about by us? How true everything around us,which we see actually has two sides - inside and outside. An aquarium, which is an ecosystem by itself. It's spectacular and so lively. Now, how much ever 'the crystal-clear glass' tank is cleaned from outside, unless inside of it is clean, it won't look so stunning and lively. How big or what colour is the seed doesn't matter. What really matters is what is inside the seed. Talking about computers, more than the outside of the computer, it is actually the inside of the computer, which matters. After you have fallen head over heels in love for the stunning looks of that new model, what really makes you own that car is the inside stuff, what's under the bonnet. Even for such an ordinary thing as buying a pair of shoes, after all the evaluation of the brand, looks, colours, style, finally it narrows down to how it feels from within.

It's the inside that really matters. Like the maxim, 'All the roads lead to Rome everything seems to be pointing at one thing. It is the inside that really matters. If so, then why do we take words (especially those words which denote negativity) literally at the face value. When a doctor says, "I'm sorry it's an incurable disease," what he actually means is, it's an 'in curable' disease and not a 'non-curable' disease. That is go within, go inside, dwell deep within you and from that higher place within you the cure is possible - 'in curable'. Moreover, you judge the way you look, you judge the way you work, you judge the way people are and you even judge how people are judging you! All the time we are judging the other end and ourselves. There comes a time in a person's life when in spite of having everything in life, he may feel incomplete. Take this as an SMS from life, telling you to get in touch with the highest force, to go within and feel complete - 'in complete'. Life is a fast track and speed is the name of the game. There may be situations wherein you feel beaten up by life. You may lose thumbs down on all grounds. You may feel incompetent. Take it a signal life telling you to go inside, dwell deep within you, meet your inner self and there will you derive a new strength, and again be ready to be competent 'in competent'. Yes, go and meet your inner self, and feel auspicious.

So only way to change your outer world is to change your inner world. If things aren't going as you want in your outer world, it is simply because things aren't going well in your inner world. All the chaos, confusions, and turmoil, which you experience in your life are just reflection of your inner cobwebs. Thus, when you experience happiness and peace all around it just means that's what you are feeling within. The outer personality is a mere reflection of inner personality. Remember it's not the outside of the balloon, but the inside of the balloon that takes it to top.

As your thoughts, as your feelings, so will be your world. What is the pointing in pointing fingers outside, and crying? Let the evil disappear and see how it evaporates, bit by bit, from the world outside too. Yes, it is the process of polishing of your inner self. Polish the mirror of life so much that one day you begin to see clearly who you are. When you see yourself, you see me and thereby feel complete.

## Chapter 25
# YOUR WORDS CREATE YOUR WORLD

# YOUR WORDS CREATE YOUR WORLD

*"Your word is your wand*

*The words you speak*

*Create your own destiny"*

— Florence Scovel Shinn

Words have the power to make or break you. Your words create the fabric of your reality. Your words are an offshoot of your thoughts, your thoughts are the by-product of your character and your character is a reflection of who you are and what you are made of. That is the impact of the words we utter. It has a bearing on our character and character will lead to destiny. Your words create your world.

## WORDS HAVE POWER:

*"Words have the power to destroy or heal. When words are both true and kind, they can change your world".*

— *Buddha*

Words have power; and when we use them in the right way, words will make miracles happen. For example, when you say, 'I don't want war'; you are giving your thought and attention to war and where you give your thought and attention, your energy will flow. The law of attraction will match your energy with that thought and bring it into your reality. So instead of saying, "I don't want war", you should say "I want peace". Then your thought and attention is on peace, so you are giving your energy to peace and the law of attraction will match your energy with peace and hence your life will be peaceful. This Universe thus works on your thoughts. In the same way, try replacing your statements as follows.

Replace "I don't want to fail" with "I want to win".

Replace "I don't want to be fat" with "I want to be slim".

Replace "I don't want to have a stressed job" with "I want to have a happy and exciting job".

Our thoughts are very powerful because energy is transmitted through our thoughts. So give utmost importance to your thoughts. If you stop talking and thinking about what you want and change your vocabulary and only think and talk about what you want, then you will start attracting what you want, and what you don't want will gradually vanish from your life. Let us remove a few bad words from our dictionary... Changing our thought pattern will help us channelize our energy and our life will change accordingly.

## POSITIVE SELF-TALK:

*"Change your thoughts and you change your world"*

— *Norman Vincent Peale*

An affirmation is a strong positive statement telling you that all is well. With constant repetition, affirmation help you drown out the negative messages of your mind. When you repeat affirmations, subtle changes occur within you, altering you for the better, the way you act and feel and the world reacts more positively to you. Whenever you are walking down the street, getting into an elevator or having a few moments alone, give yourself a mini motivational talk. One warning though— don't move your lips, or people will think you have gone mad.

I do it all the time. I take a few moments to refocus on the type of person I want to be. I get clear on my goals. I tell myself this meeting will go fantastically, or that I am a top performer. You may feel uncomfortable, talking yourself up this way, but I assure you it really works. Your brain responds to almost any command you give it up. Emphatically tell it it's happy and it will get happier. Tell your brain you are full of energy and sure enough, your energy will increase. But saying nothing to your brain all day along and pretty soon it slips back into negative thinking patterns. The trick with positive self-talk is to do it consistently. The first two weeks it will take some effort but then it will become a habit. Soon you'll become your personal coach, pepping yourself up constantly. And your energy and enthusiasm will skyrocket as a result. Remember, you are what you think about most of the time. Discipline yourself to think only constructive, empowering thoughts and your life will just get better. Let negative self-talk get hold of you and it doesn't matter how rich and successful you are, you will be miserable. I believe how we think about ourselves and how we talk ourselves are two important success factors of our entire life. It's worth the effect to get them right. When words are consecrated and chanted in a particular way, they become mantras and give power to your inner soul which will perform miracles. Use the time before you sleep. The time before you nod off and when you get up early morning is very effective in programming your subconscious mind. And fall asleep by repeating 'I feel better and better every day in every way' Use it to your benefit. Thus, you can create your own magic mantra for your well-being. "I am Positive, I am Powerful, I am Peaceful, I am Successful, I am Beautiful, I am Healthy, I am Perfect".

## YOU ARE THE SOLE ARCHITECT OF YOUR LIFE:

> *"The universe doesn't give you what you ask, for with your thoughts; it gives you what you demand with your actions"*
>
> — Dr. Steve Maraboli

Why not engineer a new life for yourself? Work with the structure you already possess and build a new "You" that is positive and makes the best and most of your talents and abilities. Take a look within yourself. In what ways do you put your finest qualities to create even something greater of yourself? In what ways do you make the most of your lesser characteristics and work with your strengths to present to the world a surprising revitalized "you". When we build ourselves and our lives using affirmative elements, we can bask in the shining accomplishment of a newer created self, standing tall in the world and strong in foundation. Move forward with only the best ingredients of thought and action you can gather and your prostration of forts will reward you mind over body. Every thought that crosses our mind or every word that we utter signals the body accordingly and the body responds by manifesting the thoughts. This is exactly why positive self-affirmations / self-talk / mantras work like magic. Not convinced about the power of mind and its connection with body? Then try this little exercise. Just before bed time close your eyes, take a few breaths, slow inhales and even slower exhales, sit with your back erect and after a few breaths start telling your subconscious mind the time you want to wake up next morning. For e.g.; whisper to yourself, "I will wake up at 5 am tomorrow". Do it couple of times to firmly tell your mind and notice how it serves you the next morning!

Each one of us has the gift of free will or the freedom to think whatever we choose to concentrate on most, throughout the day. Ask yourself right now what thoughts are you on right now? Are you thinking about lack and limitation? Your environment and your feelings will let you know exactly what you are thinking because they are exact replace of your thought and beliefs. It's time no one can think of prosperity all day long and we are in agreement there.

To get more prosperity in your life you should affirm that you are prosperous. For those of you who are not familiar with affirmations or why they are important to your success, just think of them as positive statements that we can use to change our mind, belief system, attitudes and actions and therefore get the results we want. A fabulous affirmation for prosperity would be "By day and by night, I am being prospered in all my ways". To get more prosperity in your life you should affirm that you are prosperous. As Emerson said, *"A man is what he thinks about all day long"*. Your primary thought, the once you concentrate on most, will be what you will see in the people you attract to you as well in your life circumstances. One of the most popular sayings 'change your thought and change your life', but of course Rome wasn't built in a day! It will take time to replace habitual thought that are negative to more positive ones, but you can do it! Domenic Polifrone once said, if we wanted a new car that we needed to go down to the showroom, get behind the wheel of the car and test drive it, get a few brochures to keep. See and feel yourself driving and owning this beautiful new car. Get into the consciousness of "I am prosperity and I am in the process of buying and moving the beautiful new car." Try it. This experiment works! Your mind is one of your prized possessions. It has been said that you are the architect of your life.

Ask yourself right now what kind of life are you building for yourself? A magnificent life or limited life? Everything that has been available to everyone is also available to you. There is a wonderful quote which underscores this fact. He said, "No one is superior to what you might become". Start knowing that the potentiality of one is potentiality of all. If anybody has wealth you can also have wealth. If anybody has a beautiful home, you can have a beautiful home. Life is a state of consciousness, "As a man thinks in his heart so he". Change your consciousness and change your world.

From now on use the word 'challenges' instead of 'problems'; I am feeling on Top of the world than the mundane 'Okay and fine'; 'Lessons learned' than 'failures'; 'I invest time' and not 'I spend time' and the list is endless. The quality of your vibrations is carried by your words. These vibrations affect or infect world. Unlearn the words that create unhappiness and learn the words that create celebrations. Unlearn the words that limit you and learn the words that create you. Start living with a new tongue and let our words be sweet. Your words create your world.

# Chapter 26
# ZEN AND THE SELF

# ZEN AND THE SELF

*"To study the Buddha*
*Way is to study the self.*
*To study the self is to forget the self,*
*To forget the self is to awaken to all things."*

— Zen Master Dogen

**THE ESSENCE OF SELF:**

When the mind is devoid of all its possible content, we not only find absolute serenity and peace, we also discover the true nature of self. Usually we derive our sense of self from the various things that distinguish us as individuals — our bodies and their appearance; our history; our nationality, the roles we play, our work, our social and financial status, what we own, what others think of us. We also derive an identity from the thoughts and feelings we have, from our beliefs and values, from our creative and intellectual abilities, from our character and personality. These, and many other aspects of our lives, contribute to our sense of who we are.

However, such an identity is forever at the mercy of events, forever vulnerable, and forever in need of protection and support. If anything on which our identity depends changes, or threatens to change, our very sense of self is threatened. In addition to deriving an identity from how we experience ourselves in the world, we also derive a sense of self from the very fact that we are experiencing. If there is experience, then there must be an experienced one; there must be an "I" who is doing the experiencing. What is going on in mind, there is this sense that I am the subject of it all.

But what exactly is this sense of "I-ness"? I use the word "I" hundreds of times a day without hesitation. I say that I am thinking or seeing something, that I have a feeling or desire, that I know or remember something. It is most familiar, most intimate, most oblivious aspect of myself. I know exactly what I mean by "I" - until I try to describe it or define it. Then I run into trouble.

When the mind is silent the thoughts, feelings, perceptions and memories with which we habitually identify have fallen away, then what remains is the essence of self, the pure subject without an object. What we then find is not a sense of "I am this" or "I am that", but just "I am". In this state you know the essence of self, and you know that the essence to be pure consciousness. You know this to be what you really are. This core identity has none of the uniqueness of the individual self. Beyond all attributes and identifying characteristics, your sense of I-ness is indistinguishable from mine. The light of consciousness shining in you, which you label as "I", is the same light that I label as "I". In this we are identical. I am the light. And so are you.

This essential self is eternal; it never changes. It is pure consciousness, and is the faculty of consciousness without any content. The Buddhist scholar D.T. Suzuki referred to it as a *"state of Absolute Emptiness"*. There is no time, space, becoming, nothingness. Pure experience is the mind seeing itself as reflected in itself... If you ever become serious about happiness, weary of temporary happiness slipping through your fingers time and again, then go after the missing element. The missing element is emptiness and there is a good way, a gradual way, and a certain way to bring this element into your life. This emptiness is the doorway to a new life, and the doorway to emptiness is meditation.

Zen meditation is a contemporary form of "Buddhist meditation", which can be adopted and practiced to gain eternal peace. The entire practice of Zen meditation provides immense clarity and insights into the working of mind. When the mind fully attains the state of complete quietude and drop its perceptions of sense-objects, at that stage in meditation the mind is really "no mind". To quieten the rushing thoughts is the sacred function of the yoga of meditation. And training of the mind reduces negative emotions and promotes positive feelings. Which means we have the capacity to reduce negative emotions ourselves.

## MONKEY MIND AND MINDFULNESS MEDITATION:

We tend to multi-task and divide our attention towards multiple things at a time, focusing on what we have yet to do rather than what we are currently doing. This may be compared to the temptation our monkey brains feel upon seeing many bananas on one tree. Research on mindfulness suggests that we have two different modes of mind. The 'doing' mode is focused on 'getting things done' and the 'being mode' is focused on 'letting things be'. Each mode has its own function and purpose depending on the situation. For example, the doing mode helps us achieve tasks but it will not help us fall asleep at night. Mindfulness meditation provides us with an opportunity to step in the being mode by following simple mindfulness meditation exercises. It stops the brain for a while to move away from the constant doing mode.

## ZEN MEDITATION TO SAIL THROUGH LIFE:

Zen meditation is a type of meditation that originates from the Tang Dynasty, China and is one of the highly proclaimed Buddhist traditions that is as old as 7th century. The entire practice of Zen meditation provides immense clarity and insights into working of the mind. The process of Zen meditation involves the art of observing your thoughts and feelings and then letting go in the mind. This meditation is primarily based on the power of harnessing the intuitions as compared to the logic. This meditation is a special way of connecting with the human mind and heart and becoming a Buddha. With the help of this meditation, a person becomes capable of understanding the causes of unhappiness while directing the focus to bring true understanding.

## EFFECT OF ZEN MEDITATION:

The key to real happiness lies within all of us. Zen meditation helps people to raise awareness and become interconnected with everything that life has to offer. We also start focusing on the happiness and peace of other people more and more. On an everyday level, Zen also helps the mind to increase the power of self-reflection with increased creativity and focus. It also reduces stress and anxiety, a better immune system, good sleeping pattern and other health improvements.

## HOW ZEN MEDITATION IS DONE:

- **Breath Observation**

    Zen meditation which requires sitting in an upright position while focusing on the breath. In doing so, your mind is concentrating on your body and breath and is not busy in contemplating past or future thoughts. In this way you put brake on your busy mind so that it doesn't race through thoughts, as it usually does. With this method, a sense of awareness and consciousness increase.

- **Quiet Awareness**

    In this meditation, the trick is to allow the mind to be flooded with thoughts without any rejection or unnecessary judgements. This practice is called Shikantaza in Japanese, which means to sit. This method does not require any object while allowing the mind just to be. All that one needs to do is 'be alert' to all that is happening in life. The bull within your inner self and the driver or bullhead, is the one who is commanding it to work, perform and achieve. The happiest, most synergised person is the one who does not fall into this trap of conflict between the two but works and lives in synergy. With our external world undergoing rapid and unpredictable changes, we experience lot of stress and frustration around us. Mindfulness meditation protects us from thorns of life. Simplicity is the key to mindfulness. It is not about going somewhere or getting something. It is to realise the fact, that life is not perfect and we need to face it as it happens. There is no point in being fearful about something that has happened or worry about something that has already happened. We need to focus on the present with mindfulness. By facing our fears and difficulties, we can befriend them and by befriending them we create clarity to deal with the situation in a better manner without battling between the fight or flight mode. With this clarity, you become emotionally calm, open-hearted, courageous and connected. This clarity gives you the guidance to choose the right path of life.

Printed in Great Britain
by Amazon

62558407R00175